Signs of the Times

Signs of the Times

Pastoral Translations of Ministry & Culture
in Honor of Leonard I. Sweet

Brian A. Ross, Editor

Foreword by Wayne McCown

WIPF & STOCK · Eugene, Oregon

SIGNS OF THE TIMES
Pastoral Translations of Ministry & Culture in Honor of Leonard I. Sweet

Copyright © 2016 Wipf and Stock Publishers. All rights reserved. Except for brief quotations in critical publications or reviews, no part of this book may be reproduced in any manner without prior written permission from the publisher. Write: Permissions, Wipf and Stock Publishers, 199 W. 8th Ave., Suite 3, Eugene, OR 97401.

Wipf & Stock
An Imprint of Wipf and Stock Publishers
199 W. 8th Ave., Suite 3
Eugene, OR 97401

www.wipfandstock.com

PAPERBACK ISBN: 978-1-4982-2060-6
HARDCOVER ISBN: 978-1-4982-2062-0

Manufactured in the U.S.A.

New Revised Standard Version Bible, copyright 1989, Division of Christian Education of the National Council of the Churches of Christ in the United States of America. Used by permission. All rights reserved.

Revised Standard Version of the Bible, copyright 1952 (2nd ed., 1971) by the Division of Christian Education of the National Council of the Churches of Christ in the United States of America. Used by permission. All rights reserved.

Scripture quotations from THE MESSAGE. Copyright © by Eugene H. Peterson 1993, 1994, 1995, 1996, 2000, 2001, 2002. Used by permission of Tyndale House Publishers, Inc.

Scripture quotations marked ESV are from ESV Copyright and Permissions Information The Holy Bible, English Standard Version® (ESV®) Copyright © 2001 by Crossway, a publishing ministry of Good News Publishers. All rights reserved. ESV Text ed.: 2007.

Scripture quotations marked NLT are taken from the *Holy Bible*, New Living Translation, copyright ©1996, 2004, 2007, 2013 by Tyndale House Foundation. Used by permission of Tyndale House Publishers, Inc., Carol Stream, Illinois 60188. All rights reserved.

Scripture quotations taken from the New American Standard Bible®, Copyright © 1960, 1962, 1963, 1968, 1971, 1972, 1973, 1975, 1977, 1995 by The Lockman Foundation. Used by permission. (www.Lockman.org)

Scriptures taken from the Holy Bible, New International Version®, NIV®. Copyright © 1973, 1978, 1984, 2011 by Biblica, Inc.™ Used by permission of Zondervan. All rights reserved worldwide. www.zondervan.com The "NIV" and "New International Version" are trademarks registered in the United States Patent and Trademark Office by Biblica, Inc.®

Contents

List of Contributors | vii

Foreword by Wayne McCown | ix

Sweet & the Spirit: An Introduction to Semiotician Leonard I. Sweet | xiii
Brian A. Ross

1   Summoned to Follow: Leonard Sweet's Antidote for the Leadership Cult | 1
Anthony L. Blair

2   Wake Up and Smell the Future: From Post-Christian to Post-Church | 20
Jason Clark

3   Preaching as Bricolage | 33
Charles J. Conniry Jr.

4   Heretics and the Way Forward | 42
Dottie Escobedo-Frank

5   What's Going on Here? Trusting God's Story in Your Own | 53
Dwight J. Friesen

Contents

6   The EPIC World of Anglican Worship | 65
Todd Hunter

7   Every Bush is Burning | 77
Thomas E. Ingram

8   Indefinable | 96
Dan Kimball

9   Identity, Vocation, and Calling | 100
David McDonald

10   Rearranging the Furniture of Faith | 117
Mike McNichols

11   EPIC Parenting in the Post-Church Church | 131
Rich Melheim

12   Discovering the Future, Hidden Deep within the Past | 146
Brian A. Ross

13   Reading Signs: Serving Families Affected by Disability | 162
Christine Roush

14   An Epistemology of Empathy | 177
Jeff Tacklind

Contributors

Anthony L. Blair, President, Dean of the Faculty, and Professor of Leadership and Historical Studies at the Evangelical Theological Seminary, Myerstown, Pennsylvania.

Jason Clark, Founding Pastor of Vineyard Church Sutton, London, and Lead Mentor for the Leadership and Global Perspectives DMin at the George Fox Evangelical Seminary, Portland, Oregon.

Charles J. Conniry, Jr., Vice President and Dean of the George Fox Evangelical Seminary, Portland, Oregon.

Dottie Escobedo-Frank, District Superintendent of the Desert Southwest Conference of The United Methodist Church.

Dwight J. Friesen, Associate Professor of Practical Theology at the Seattle School of Theology and Psychology.

Todd Hunter, Founding Bishop of the Diocese of Churches for the Sake of Others and Founding Pastor of Holy Trinity Anglican Church in Costa Mesa.

Thomas E. Ingram, Chief Dreamer at crowdsourcingchristianity.com and Linen Publishing, Master Gardener with the Tulsa County Extension of the Oklahoma State University.

Contributors

Dan Kimball, Professor/Director of the ReGeneration Project at the Western Seminary, Portland, Oregon, and on staff at Vintage Faith Church, Santa Cruz.

David McDonald, Lead Pastor at Westwinds Community Church, Jackson, Michigan, and Post-Doctoral Fellow, at the George Fox Evangelical Seminary, Portland, Oregon.

Mike McNichols, Director of the Fuller Theological Seminary's regional campus in Irvine, California, and Affiliate Assistant Professor of Intercultural Studies.

Rich Melheim, Founder, CEO, and Chief Creative Officer of Faith Inkubators and the RICH Learning Preschool Incubators Project.

Brian A. Ross, Assistant Professor of Pastoral Ministries at the Fresno Pacific Biblical Seminary and Adjunct Professor at the Toccoa Falls College, Georgia.

Christine Roush, COO and VP of Advancement at Rainbow Acres, Camp Verde, Arizona.

Jeff Tacklind, Lead Pastor at the Laguna Evangelical Free Church.

Foreword

I MAY BE THINKING of myself more highly than I ought! But I think Len would agree: I served as both a scholarly and spiritual mentor during his years as an undergraduate student. Not in the role of an academic advisor or major professor. I was "only" his Sunday School teacher!

Many years ago now, my wife Darlene and I moved from Seattle, Washington, to Richmond, Virginia. Having just completed her master's in Nursing Education, Darlene immediately went to work as faculty at the Medical College of Virginia. Soon after we settled into a student apartment at Union Theological Seminary, where I had been admitted for doctoral studies. Those tasks accomplished, our next was to locate a "church home." Within the month, we decided on a small Wesleyan church, based particularly on the welcome of the pastor and his wife.

We had only attended this church a few weeks when Pastor Ken came to our apartment and asked if we would teach a "college class." He explained that he expected two students from New York to be returning soon to resume their studies at the University of Richmond. The next Sunday morning we met them: Leonard and his younger brother Philip (now professor of German at the University of Radford).

These two young men (I think, at the time, both still teenagers) would form the core of our Sunday School class. But as Darlene and I thought and prayed about this opportunity, we struck on the idea of expanding it and calling it the "The College and Young Professionals Class," to include young professionals (like Darlene). Pastor Ken supported this idea, as well as our proposal that we meet in the Byrd Park gazebo directly across the street

Foreword

from the church. This meeting place provided us a more informal setting where we could gather around coffee and donuts (which were not allowed in the church).

I served as the primary teacher. Both Len and Phil faithfully attended the class (I do not recall them missing a single Sunday, except during academic holidays). On occasion, they brought other students from the University of Richmond. Darlene invited her new friends at the Medical College of Virginia. Over time, this Sunday School class grew to more than 50, larger than the congregation across the street, a development that proved problematic for some of the church members. We decided to discontinue the class when Len completed his BA degree.

Already in his youth, Leonard Sweet evidenced a wide range of talents and versatility at multi-tasking. He served as director of our church choir. Simultaneously he provided the piano accompaniment, sang a part, and directed the choir. This amazed me; early on, I concluded that Len was a genius.

During our years together in Richmond, Len and Phil were regularly in our apartment at Union Theological Seminary, especially on weekends. Our personal lives became interlaced . . . and that has continued to this day, although not in such close proximity. Len would go on to earn his MDiv and PhD degrees in Rochester, NY, where Darlene and I have lived for the past 25+ years. He earned his PhD at the University of Rochester, where Darlene served as Academic Dean and Professor in the School of Nursing. I spent the last 20 years of my full-time working career on the campus of Roberts Wesleyan College, where (a little known fact!) Len began college as a freshman before transferring to the University of Richmond. I also was privileged to found on the Roberts' campus Northeastern Seminary, a sister school to Colgate Rochester Divinity School, where Len earned his MDiv and later served as Provost and Professor of Church History.

There are further linkages. Len was raised in the Free Methodist Church; his mother (who was very influential in his spiritual upbringing) was a preacher. As a college student, I joined the Free Methodist Church and became an ordained minister. Later, I served for 12 years as Professor of Biblical Studies and for eight years as the Dean at George Fox (formerly Western) Evangelical Seminary, where since 2001 Len has served as a Distinguished Visiting Professor.

During the past four decades, Leonard Sweet has distinguished himself not only as a professor (at several institutions), but also as an author, preacher and public speaker. Len has been able to do all of these things simultaneously, or at least in moving from one to the next, quite seamlessly. Moreover, he has excelled in all of these areas, and his output in each has been prolific.

Len was educated as an historian and has held several posts in Church History. But, over time, he has become more widely known as a futurist. Personally, he prefers to describe his calling in ministry using the (Anglicized) Greek term *semeiotics*. (Len pushes his hearers/readers beyond the boundaries of normal vocabulary, frequently creating new words to express his ideas.) *Semeiotics*, as practiced by Len, is sufficiently explained by Brian Ross in the Introduction to this volume. I want to introduce in this foreword a familiar but new descriptor to characterize Leonard Sweet (this is the kind of thing Len himself would do!).

I believe Leonard Sweet is a prophet.

The prophets of the Old Testament evidence a personal familiarity with the history and traditions of Israel. Their "word from the LORD" assumes this history; it is foundational to their prophetic message. Amos, for example, references "the law of the LORD" and "his statutes" in preaching to Israel (2:4). He recites the exodus from Egypt, destruction of the Amorite, forty years in the wilderness, and possession of the (promised) land (2:9–10). However, he also shocks his audience by "turning on its head" the prevailing interpretation of Israel's religious history: "Hear this word that the LORD has spoken against you, O people of Israel, against the whole family that I brought up out of the land of Egypt: You only have I known of all the families of the earth; *therefore I will punish you for all your iniquities*" (3:1–2, highlight added). All of this looks a lot like we get from Len Sweet!

While many assume all prophecy is predictive, biblical scholars have concluded that at least 80 percent of the messages in the OT books of prophecy address current events. Based on present realities, viewed theologically and spiritually, the prophets speak concerning future prospects. Here's one example (which could be multiplied a hundredfold): "They hate the one who reproves in the gate, and they abhor the one who speaks the truth. Therefore because you trample on the poor and take from them levies of grain, you have built houses of hewn stone, but you shall not live in them; you have planted pleasant vineyards, but you shall not drink their wine . . . Seek good and not evil, that you may live; and so the LORD, the God of hosts will be with you, just as you have said. Hate evil and love good, and establish justice in the gate; it may be that the LORD, the God of hosts, will be gracious to the remnant of Joseph" (Amos 5:10-11. 14-15). Often, that's the kind of message Len Sweet delivers: "The word is out: Reinvent yourself for the 21st century or die" (*Soul Tsunami*)!

I believe Len is a modern-day prophet a lot like the OT prophet Habakkuk. In Habakkuk 1, the prophet expresses his consternation at the situation that obtains among the people of God (for Leonard, it is the contemporary church). They seem oblivious to what is happening around them . . . but the prophet is not. He sees signs (*semeiotics*!) on the horizon. He works at understanding what God is up to, and what the future portends for his people. This book (like many of Len's) makes extensive use of imagery in communicating its message. It climaxes with "a prayer of the prophet Habakkuk," a prayer echoed across Len's life work and ministry: "O LORD, I have heard of your renown, and I stand in awe, O LORD, of your work. In our time revive it; in our own time make it known" (3:1-2).

Along with the authors in this volume, I thank God for giving the contemporary church such a gifted prophet. But I also thank Leonard Sweet for his "long obedience in the same direction" (Eugene Peterson) and for his commitment to Jesus. At the close of his 2007 "Response to Misunderstandings," Len declared: "I only want to write one thing over the doorpost to my heart and life: 'Jesus Christ lives here.'" Me too, my friend.

Wayne McCown, PhD

Provost Emeritus, Roberts Wesleyan College
Founding Dean Emeritus, Northeastern Seminary
President, Friends of Hope Africa University

Sweet & the Spirit
An Introduction to Semiotician Leonard I. Sweet

Brian A. Ross, DMin

> He replied, "When evening comes, you say, 'It will be fair weather, for the sky is red,' and in the morning, 'Today it will be stormy, for the sky is red and overcast.' You know how to interpret the appearance of the sky, but you cannot interpret the signs of the times."
>
> —*Matthew 16:2–3 NIV*

> For as I walked around and looked carefully at your objects of worship, I even found an altar with this inscription: to an unknown god. So you are ignorant of the very thing you worship—and this is what I am going to proclaim to you . . .
> "For in him we live and move and have our being." As some of your own poets have said, "We are his offspring."
>
> —*Acts 17:23; 28*

> Dear friends, do not believe every spirit, but test the spirits to see whether they are from God.
>
> —*1 John 4:1*

For several decades, Leonard Ira Sweet, PhD, has worked to follow the Spirit of Jesus,

> "Seeing things the rest of us do not see, and dreaming possibilities that are beyond most of our imagining. As a writer, preacher,

professor, and consultant, he communicates the gospel with a signature bridging of the worlds of faith, academe, and popular culture." [1]

Leonard Sweet is a graduate of the University of Richmond, Colgate Rochester Divinity School, and the University of Rochester. An ordained United Methodist minister, Sweet served as Provost of Colgate Rochester/Bexley Hall/Crozier Divinity School while still in his twenties. For nine years he was the President and Professor of Church History at United Theological Seminary (at the time of his appointment, he was the youngest seminary president in North America.) For six years, Sweet was Dean of the Drew Theological School and Vice President of Drew University, where he currently holds the position of E. Stanley Jones Professor of Evangelism. Since 2001, he has been a Distinguished Visiting Professor at George Fox University and beginning in 2014, Sweet was named the Distinguished Visiting Professor of Graduate Theological Education at Tabor College.

But despite this vast and varied C.V., Len is mainly known as original thinker, who prayerfully muses over the current state and future possibilities for the church of Jesus Christ. Many have encountered his vision through the more than two-hundred articles, one-thousand three-hundred published sermons, and more than fifty books he has authored.

Len comes from humble, yet Jesus-soaked beginnings. Raised in poverty in the hills of West Virginia, he was blessed to be raised in the faith by his fiery preacher mother. In his dedication to her in his book, *A Cup of Coffee at the Soul Café*, Len writes:

> Here's to Mabel Boggs Sweet, who raised three boys in the poorest section of a town (a street called 'Hungry Hill'), who expected 'her boys' to get an education without any money to help them get that education (all three of whom went on to get Ph.D's), and whose philosophy of child-rearing was simple: 'I'm not going to isolate you boys from the world, but I am going to insulate you,' and who herself home-schooled her sons in Christianity while she sent us to the public schools. [2]

Rev. Mabel Sweet, and by extension his family as a whole, did not have it easy. As an early female minister, she and her boys were subject to much ridicule and false accusations. Though anything but liberal (Len says his Mother regularly spoke to him and his brothers about "What Jesus

---

1. "Leonard Sweet Biography," *Spirit Venture Ministries*.
2. Sweet, *Cup of Coffee*, dedication.

told me") the family was often on the outs with the church due to supposedly "worldly" behavior like having watched a television program. From his childhood, largely through the example of his mother, Len was engrained with a deep, Jesus-centered faith. However, part of this faith involved calling the church to pay attention to the future that the Spirit was ushering in and not to merely cling to a form of dead religion from yesteryear.

Though initially desiring to serve as a traditional church historian, eventually, Len sensed a call from the Spirit to the ministry of *semiotics*. In an online interview Sweet explained his vocation:

> The Greek word for "signs" is *semeion*, and semiotics is the study of signs and the art of making connections, seeing the relationships between apparently random signs and reading the meaning of those relationships.
>
> Our brains are designed to detect patterns. So I only do what everyone else can do if we do what we're designed to do . . .
>
> Disciples of Jesus must learn to read the sign-language of the Spirit. Sometimes God gives us a hint; sometimes God drops a hammer on us. But the handwriting is on the wall. God's finger is still writing. Can we read the signs of what God is doing? The ultimate in spiritual illiteracy is the inability to read the handwriting on the wall, especially when the essence of evangelism is announcing the good sign, the Jesus Sighting. For me, semiotics is another way of talking about the signs of the Spirit's activity in the world. For we are sent into the world to join Jesus in his continuing mission.
>
> Also—there are some people in the church preoccupied with reading signs, but they're looking only for one thing: not signs of our times, but end times signs, signs of the coming of Christ, signs of the "latter days" and the "end of days." I'm trying, instead, to read the signs which give us Jesus sightings.[3]

In a personal conversation with Len at a greasy spoon in Central Pennsylvania, I asked him what he considers to be his specific academic expertise. For example, N.T. Wright specializes in the history of Second Temple Judaism; Mark Noll specializes in the history of Christianity in North America; Catherine Pickstock specializes in postmodern philosophy to reinterpret premodern theology, etc. Len's response?

---

3. Sweet, "On Signs, Signals, Churches."

"My academic specialty is NOT having an academic specialty. I read and learn broadly, from various subjects, to try to discern what the Spirit is up to in the world."

This IS the work of Jesus-centered semiotics: reading, and watching, and listening broadly, to interpret the signs of the times. To have an open eye, open ear, and open heart to what the Spirit of God is up to in our world. And then working to translate it and make it known to His church.

You could say that the goal of this book is to go one level deeper: to translate the ideas and visions of Leonard Sweet, in even clearer language, to contemporary church leaders.

All of the contributors to this volume have been involved with the Doctor of Ministry program at George Fox Evangelical Seminary personally studying with Len. Many are pastors. A few are seminary professors. At least one contributor is the leader of a Christian non-profit organization. Our goal in this book is not merely to personally honor Leonard Sweet for his role as our teacher, mentor, and friend. Our primary goal is to help clarify his work, and its implications, for other church leaders who serve Jesus in everyday contexts, where ordinary people seek to follow Him in the midst of a rapidly changing world.

If we can, to some degree, reach this goal . . . it would be the greatest honor we could personally bestow on Len and his calling— one who attempts to interpret the Signs of the Times, and even more, the Signs of the Spirit.

Bibliography

"Leonard Sweet Biography." *Spirit Venture Ministries*. http://leonardsweet.com/about.
Sweet, Leonard. *A Cup of Coffee at the Soul Café: Finding the Energy of a Deeper Spiritual Life*. Nashville: Broadman & Holman, 1998.
———. "On Signs, Signals, Churches and the Current State of Starbucks." Interview by Jon M. Sweeney. http://www.explorefaith.org/faces/my_faith/leonard_sweet.php.

1

Summoned to Follow
Leonard Sweet's Antidote for the Leadership Cult

Anthony L. Blair, PhD, DMin

> Jesus called them together and said, "You know that the rulers of the Gentiles lord it over them, and their high officials exercise authority over them. Not so with you. Instead, whoever wants to become great among you must be your servant."
>
> —Matthew 20:25–26 NIV

Maxwell's House

"EVERYTHING RISES AND FALLS on leadership." So says John Maxwell, the Wesleyan pastor turned leadership guru who has now become the world's top seller of leadership literature. His organization claims to have trained over three million leaders in forty-seven languages in one hundred countries.[1] But he's not the only one saying that leadership is the sole or most critical factor affecting ministry. I have heard this mantra since my own days as a young pastor—from bishops and peers who were convinced that there was a crisis in the church (and in the world) that only strong, personality driven leadership could solve.

Over the past generation or so, Western Christians have embraced and attempted to sanctify the dominant models of leadership in our

---

1. See Eliason, "Life of Leadership."

society without much reflection and very little critique. The illustrations are ubiquitous:

- *Leadership Journal*, a Christianity Today, Inc., organ, advertises itself as "the premier publication for today's church" and has a readership of approximately eighty thousand.[2] It is accompanied by a popular blog and an electronic newsletter, and provides quarterly advice for leading churches and other ministries.

- The Global Leadership Summit, sponsored by the Willow Creek Association, attracts more than one hundred and seventy thousand leaders from around the world. It's billed as a "world-class leadership event," and includes a fascinating mixture of evangelical leaders and others whose faith commitments are either unknown or "secular" in some respect.[3]

- Perhaps no academic discipline has received more attention from Christian institutions of higher learning over the past decade than Leadership Studies. New programs have been multiplying at nearly every degree level. I am familiar with this pattern from personal experience; as a higher education administrator I have personally created or instigated the development of at least four of these programs myself (in part to offer a distinctly countercultural understanding of leadership). And I have seen nearly every other institution with which I am personally familiar do the same because of the market for these studies.

- The title "senior pastor" is in the process of becoming blasé. First, larger churches created the title of "executive pastor" for what is, essentially, the chief operating officer of the multimillion-dollar corporations that many congregations have become. And now "lead pastor" has come into vogue as a descriptor of the chief executive officers of those organizations, particularly those that are emphasizing the leadership aspect of the pastoral role.

- Undoubtedly the most popular model of leading change among American Christians is that of John Kotter of Harvard University, popularized in his book *Leading Change*. This model of leading change is top-down, linear, and dependent on motivating key followers to embrace a leader-delivered vision. Other models that place

2. "Help and Info: About Us," *Leadership Journal*, http://www.christianitytoday.com/le/help/aboutus/ourmedia.html.

3. "Global Leadership Summit," Willow Creek Association, http://www.willowcreek.com/events/leadership.

less emphasis on the leader and more emphasis on the people in the organization or community, such as the appreciative inquiry model developed by David Cooperrider of Case Western Reserve University, have been largely ignored by the church.[4]

- As a seminary president, the drumbeat I hear from both denominational leaders and from local churches is that seminaries should do better at training future pastors in leadership skills. I hear only occasional concern about the kind of character our graduates will have, very little concern about their theological commitments or assumptions, and almost no concern about the hermeneutical or homiletical skills. The most common question is, "Do they know how to grow a church"?

I could offer other examples or illustrations, of course, but these should suffice to demonstrate what the reader already knows or suspects about the importance of leadership in Western Christianity. It is about the careful acquisition and strategic use of power. It is about the person or persons at the top of the pyramid. It's about changing things for the better. It is about everything rising or falling on leadership.

This is the house that Maxwell built. And Leonard Sweet is having none of it:

> Leadership literature has been a cannibal galaxy in the church for the past forty years, gobbling up everything in its path. The leadership cannibal galaxy is so strong it will be hard for many of you to hear these words. Thinking of your faith in leadership terms has simply come to sound normal. And that's no accident. A mountain range—or more accurately, a Himalayan heap—of secondary literature on leadership has been written convinced you to think that way. The only Christian books to sell more than leadership in the past thirty years were "left behind" theologies of escape and "up your behind" theologies of wealth.[5]

Shackleton's Ship

To understand the strong emotion in that quotation, we need to appreciate Sweet's early and prophetic evaluation of the patterns noted above. He addressed the topic at some length in two books published eight years apart.

4. Cooperrider, *Appreciative Inquiry*.
5. Sweet, *I Am a Follower*, 25.

The first was 2004's *Summoned to Lead*, which introduced Ernest Shackleton, the intrepid Antarctic explorer, as a model of the kind of leadership Sweet believes God is summoning in our own time. In that volume, Sweet began a critique of the dominant leadership models of Western culture, a critique he deepened and expanded in *I Am a Follower* in 2012. Together, they represent not only a surprisingly strong and helpful assessment of the leadership cult of Western society but also a thesis in motion, as the arguments of the latter book are more fully developed than those of the former. I have therefore used a combination of their titles as the heading for this chapter.

In these two volumes, I see Sweet articulating and providing support for four primary theses:

1. leadership is about hearing (a summons), not seeing (a vision);
2. leadership is about following, not controlling;
3. leadership is about the kingdom of God, not success; and
4. leadership is about character, not charisma or competence.

Each of these represents, I hasten to suggest, an artificial dichotomy against which some readers will push back, and such nuancing is offered at the end of this chapter by way of critique and application. However, Sweet's purpose in setting them in such stark contrast is understandable: he wants to wake the American church from our sleepy compliance with values we dare not hold and patterns we should never have emulated.

Leadership is about hearing (a summons), not seeing (a vision)

"Leadership is an acoustical art."[6]

The distinction here between hearing and seeing is not intended to distract from Sweet's repeated insistence on a multisensory approach to life, worship, and even evangelism. (See, for instance, his book *Nudge* for the latter.) Rather, the difference is between hearkening to a call to action and claiming a special knowledge of the divine will for a particular community of faith. "Failure to probe the currency of hearing as well as the currency of seeing

---

6. Sweet, *Summoned to Lead*, 17.

is one reason why leadership remains one of the most studied and least understood phenomenon of the last century."[7]

He illustrates this at some length by recounting the story of Shackleton, whose ship, ironically named *Endurance*, was crushed by sea ice during his attempted trans-Antarctic expedition in 1915, leaving Shackleton and his men trapped on the ice for nearly two years. Shackleton distinguished himself by the survival of every single man of his party in that most inhospitable of environments, even as he failed to accomplish his stated objective.

> For Sir Earnest Shackleton, it was the ears. Called by colleagues "the greatest leader who ever came on God's earth, bar none," the Antarctic explorer Shackleton understood that leadership was more than meets the eye. To adapt Paschal [sic]: the ear has its reasons that the eye knows nothing of. The ability to find one's voice and to hear and call other voices into harmonious sound is the essence of a Shackleton-inspired definition of leadership as the acoustical art of imagining the future.[8]

This is why, I suggest, that how a leader understands the process of leading transformational change is not merely a question of best practices (that which defines excellence in any endeavor) but also reflects one's assumptions about the way God works in the world. The Kotter method of top-down, "visionary" leadership assumes that privileged individuals are invited into some kind of gnosis, a special knowledge of God's intents, and these individuals must be followed, much as the Renaissance notion of the divine right of kings made political rebellion not only crime but heresy. In our own time, philosopher Alastair MacIntyre has argued that bureaucrats and managers of the modern organization are granted power because of their supposed competence; they know things or can do things that ordinary people do not know or cannot do. But these claims to extraordinary competence, divine vision, or special knowledge are seldom challenged, are largely unprovable, and are, indeed, often false.[9]

If, however, the Spirit of God is incarnate with the community of his people, if the church is truly an earthly manifestation of that divine community of love we call the Trinity, then the loving will of God can best be discerned, can best be *heard*, by listening to the collective voices of the community, rather than merely its leader(s). Interestingly, appreciative inquiry

---

7. Ibid.
8. Ibid., 18.
9. See MacIntyre, *After Virtue*.

as method seeks to do this; the leader's function is to ask questions, to listen intently to the stories that arise, to call forth the best of the community's history and identity, and then to speak into existence what emerges from the process. It's a bottom-up approach to change, rather than top-down. This stance also seems consonant with a biblical understanding of community: "There are different kinds of gifts, but the same Spirit distributes them. There are different kinds of service, but the same Lord. There are different kinds of working, but in all of them and in everyone it is the same God at work" (1 Cor 12:4–6).

Sweet has not, to my knowledge, explicitly engaged these or other models of change leadership but the principle he sets forth here does lead us in a direction that can simultaneously make a leader more heroic and more humble, more loved and more loving, more responsive and more responsible. If we who are leaders were to spend less energy concocting a preferred vision of the future for our followers, we might be better able to hear their voices . . . and in, under, and through them, even the voice of the Spirit, who is the One who leads us forward. And having heard, and having gained confidence in the hearing, there is, under the right circumstances, the potential for a Shackleton to emerge in each of us.

Leadership is about following, not controlling.

"You and I are never leaders, only followers."[10]

"Come, follow me," Jesus said, "and I will send you out to fish for people" (Mark 1:17).

"As he walked along, he saw Levi son of Alphaeus sitting at the tax collector's booth. 'Follow me,' Jesus told him, and Levi got up and followed him" (Mark 2:14).

"Then he called the crowd to him along with his disciples and said: 'Whoever wants to be my disciple must deny themselves and take up their cross and follow me'" (Mark 8:34).

"Jesus looked at him and loved him. 'One thing you lack,' he said. 'Go, sell everything you have and give to the poor, and you will have treasure in heaven. Then come, follow me'" (Mark 10:21).

---

10. Sweet, *I Am a Follower*, 27.

Twenty-one times the Gospels record Jesus saying, "Follow me." And, as Sweet points out, nowhere does Jesus explicitly tell someone to lead. His imperatives are not those of power but of self-denial and nurturing:

"Feed my sheep."

"Take up your cross."

"Believe in me."

"Love one another."

Our culture, our church, has it backward, and it is doubtless because following is harder than leading. Following means taking up that cross and actually suffering, as Jesus did. It means dying, because it is only through dying that we live the new life. "'Unless a kernel of wheat falls to the ground and dies, it remains only a single seed. But if it dies, it produces many seeds,' Jesus said" (John 12:24). So it is hard for us to follow Jesus there. It is hard for us to descend like him who made himself nothing, and became a servant, becoming obedient unto death. But it is only through death that we can know resurrection. It is only through emptying that we can be full. And it is only through following that we can arrive at our true destination. This is the path of all disciples, but leaders especially. How can we trust someone with power who has never been so broken, who has never thus died? How can we follow a leader who has not followed Jesus in the path of suffering?

Follow me, Jesus insists, not into positions of power and influence, but into the margins and mangers; not into the secrets of success and celebrity, but into faith-filled "failure" and the delights of diminishment. Follow me, he invites, and though the road is narrow and the gate is not wide, there is life on the journey and not merely at the destination. Follow me, he urges, and I will make you not just fishers of men but also shepherds . . . not merely those who eat but also those who feed. Follow me, he calls, and I will lead you somewhere you did not intend to go and when you arrive, you will know that you are, at long last, at home. Follow him, for this is the only path he has given us.

The Western church has so abrogated this message of radical surrender as to glorify and sanctify its exact opposite, argues Sweet. How did we get it so wrong? He suggests two reasons: the supposed charismatic leadership of Jesus and the celebrity culture in which we find ourselves. The first reason is fairly quickly dispatched, for Jesus' practice of leadership is so much at odds with the kind of leadership espoused in the books we are reading and the conferences we are attending. He failed miserably to keep his own followers. If Jesus intended to draw people by force of personality, he was pretty bad at it.

Rather, the celebrity culture of the West, Sweet suggests, is more explanatory. "It's fair to ask: How many of us are finding our narrative identity in the stories of Christian celebrities and not in the stories of Christ?"[11] He amplifies:

> Can you see the difference between the familiar leadership model and the followership we are called to as Christians?
>
> A Jesus follower is wise: he shuts his mouth.
>
> A Jesus follower is strong: she folds her arms.
>
> A Jesus follower is assertive: he turns the other cheek.
>
> It is time we owned up to the false category of leader and its idolatry.
>
> Leadership is a function. Followership is an identity.[12]

Leadership is about the kingdom of God, not success

> *"The first question in a followership culture is this: Is it different among us?"*[13]

One can rather easily trace the historical development of the institution of the American pastorate. In the colonial era the pastor served primarily as the "village theologian," preaching and teaching the truths of God to a largely illiterate congregation. In the nineteenth century he became also a "spiritual physician," tending to the needs in a manner that we now call pastoral care. In the generation following World War II clergy were increasingly expected to serve as "pastoral counselors," and were trained accordingly. And for the past generation or so, since the baby boomer generation assumed prominence, a pastor has also been required to be "CEO."[14] It is

---

11. Ibid., 30.
12. Ibid., 34.
13. Ibid., 33.
14. It is interesting how images of Jesus have changed to accommodate this shift in understanding of clergy leadership. A "Managerial Jesus" was promoted in books such as Bruce Barton's *The Man Nobody Knows* (Bobbs-Merrill, 1925), which presented Jesus as the first-century equivalent of a corporate executive; see also Laurie Beth Jones's *Jesus CEO* (MJF, 1995) and Larry Julian's *God Is My CEO* (Adams, 2001).

interesting to note that the previous expectations have not decreased, only that new ones have been added. And so the typical pastor of an American church in the twenty-first century is expected to preach as well as the "competition" on television or the internet; to care wisely, gently, and competently for one's parishioners as they encounter the vicissitudes of life; to counsel with insight and knowledge regarding the thorny issues of life in a broken world; to successfully lead a complex organization, including mastery of finance, marketing, and personnel management skills; and to be a visionary, attractive leader who will draw people to his or her personality and thus grow the church larger each year.

Many drop out. Many continue laboring on in frustration and guilt, concluding that they do not have what it takes to do what God has called them to do but lacking other tangible options. Some wisely opt instead for what are now called "staff positions" and specialize in an area of ministry for which they have some particular gifting or passion. Some succeed in meeting most of these expectations, and impose the same burden on those coming after. Was this what Jesus intended? When he preached that the kingdom of God was among us, did he imagine that we would someday measure it in terms of Sunday morning worship attendance, the size of the auditoriums and parking lots in which the faithful gather, the ratio of revenue to expense in the church budget, and the amount of staff on our roster? Is this addiction to "bigger, better, and faster" what it is all about? Did he envision that we would sidle up to the Herods of our day and invite their input on building our temples and manipulating the masses?

Leonard Sweet says no. He decries the ABC (attendance, buildings, and cash) metrics of success in the American church and the Wall Street methods of attaining it.

> We have been presumptuous enough to believe that the techniques and methods of the business world will adequately equip us to battle and powers and principalities of the world . . . So pastors and church leaders arm themselves by devouring books and articles on leadership and organizational strategy and structure written by men and women who have shaped the Wall Street world of business and finance. We turn to organizational gurus and White House speechwriters to teach us about serving in the kingdom of the Lord of lords. Seriously? We fly hundreds, even thousands of miles and pay big bucks to learn from Fortune 500 CEOS about how to lead the church that is bought and paid for

with the blood of the One who modeled leadership by humbling himself as a lowly servant? Really?[15]

Really. So perhaps is it time that we renew our imaginations about what the kingdom of God really entails. Perhaps this is our moment to forsake our perpetual pursuit of respectability and our passionate longing for success. Perhaps it will be the wisdom of this generation to choose "smaller, simpler, and slower" over "bigger, better, faster." The kingdom of God, Jesus said, would be marked by blessings for those at the margins: the poor, the meek, those who mourn, the gentle, those who hunger and thirst for justice, those without agenda, the peaceful and persecuted ones. How many of these phrases make it into the position descriptions or advertisements for leadership roles in Christian churches or organizations? Perhaps it is time that this changes. Really.

Leadership is about character, not charisma or competence

> *"The church has always had music. What it has lacked is leaders who know how to musick."*[16]

The distinction Sweet is making here is between those who, on the one hand, can "go with the flow," who can get lost in the modulations of the Spirit, who can keep dancing when the tempo changes, and those, on the other hand, who subject all enterprises to strategic plans and fixed processes.

> The planning mode leads to dissonance. The modulation mode leads to consonance. The challenge of voice-activated leadership is to move from the planning mode to the modulation mode, to move from dissonance to consonance, from linear thinking to lateral thinking. In modern times we focused on salvation through processes and planning. Any action must come out of a "long range" plan that established long-term goals and objectives. Before any concrete steps are taken there must be a "strategic plan" and, behind it, "action plans" and "backup plans." Our view of the future was based on "feasibility studies" and the plans we controlled (or at least though we did).[17]

---

15. Sweet, *I Am a Follower*, 88.
16. Sweet, *Summoned*, 175.
17. Ibid., 176.

I have taught strategic thinking and planning for years and am tempted to quibble a bit. There is undoubtedly an unfair dichotomy here between planning and "modulation," but I do get his point: Those who claim to live by the Spirit must lead by the Spirit. And the Spirit will almost always surprise us. The Spirit will lead us into places we would not otherwise go, will invite us into adventures we would not otherwise risk, and will ask of us sacrifices we would not otherwise make. This theme is not unique to Sweet, of course. Gordon T. Smith notes that "suffering, setbacks and disappointments are the very means by which we are formed into people of maturity and strength."[18] And this is one of the major themes of popular Franciscan spiritual teacher Richard Rohr: that the path to resurrection is the road to the cross, that pain is a necessary part of the journey, and that those who do not transform their pain will certainly transmit it.[19] So why do it? Sweet encourages that, if we dare the journey, the Spirit will also teach us new songs of hope and new dances of joy to accompany them.

The Spirit will descend upon those who least expect it, and summon them to show the rest of us where God is already at work. Planning cannot do this for us; only Spirit-led preparedness can make us ready for the summons. And preparedness is a work of character, not charisma or competence. Most of the models and theories of leadership effectiveness developed in the West over the past half century or so have emphasized the latter two attributes at the expense of the first. These studies have not been without benefit; through them we have learned what skills to utilize when, what relational approaches to take in which situations, which leadership characteristics to seek for any given job, how leaders can motivate subordinates to accomplish objectives, how leaders can mentor subordinates, and how to quantify effectiveness. But none of them have taught us character, much less the character that is forged through long practice in trusting the Spirit.

The dominant theories of our own generation do a bit better, as they offer us some moral idealism instead of the amorality of mere effectiveness. The transformational leadership model encourages us to engage in leadership actions that will positively transform followers, as well as the organization.[20] The servant leadership model invites us to take a different

---

18. Smith, *Courage and Calling*, 145.

19. See particularly *Falling Upward: A Spirituality for the Two Halves of Life* (Jossey-Bass, 2011).

20. See James MacGregor Burns, *Leadership* (HarperCollins, 1978), and Bernard Bass and Ronald E. Riggio, *Transformational Leadership*, 2nd ed. (Psychology Press, 2005).

stance toward those with whom we work.[21] Both have much to commend themselves, but both can be manipulated. The transformational model has made life more difficult for those who lack the charisma of those rare individuals who have been touted as its primary examples. How can a mere mundane mortal compete with Gandhi and King, if that is what leadership requires? And the servant leadership model is now being marketed as a tool of organizational effectiveness, so that one is encouraged to act like a servant to motivate, or even manipulate, one's followers, rather than simply because it is right. If servant leadership were not more deemed effective than another style, would we do it anyway?

So charisma and competence are not sufficient for the kingdom of God. Sometimes they even get in the way. Sweet argues that one of the things wrong with the "planning model" is that it over-emphasizes the self: "We expect to self-pilot our way into the future. The hyphenated self was the pride and joy of modernity—self-help, self-power, self-service—but it was also the end of wisdom and wonder. The harder we work at controlling our environment, the more we feel that we are less and less on top of things than ever before. Because we are."[22] It is time, he suggests, to yield control to the Spirit and be prepared for real life, in whatever form it comes.

This was the secret of Ernest Shackleton's inspirational leadership. He planned "merely" to cross the Antarctic; he failed at this but, because he knew how to "musick," became immortalized as a hero for the ages.

Sweet's Summons

The day I first met Leonard Sweet was in a doctor of ministry class at George Fox Evangelical Seminary. Our cohort gathered in a circle and we introduced ourselves at some length to our new "celebrity instructor." When we were finished, he rose from his seat, went to the door, and summoned us to follow: "Let's go see a movie!" And so we did. We hopped into our cars and drove to a local theatre to watch *Open Range*, the 2003 Western with Kevin Costner, Robert Duvall, and Annette Bening. The point of the exercise was

---

21. See Robert Greenleaf, *Servant Leadership: A Journey into the Nature of Legitimate Power and Greatness*, 25th anniv. ed. (Paulist, 2002); Larry C. Spears and Michele Lawrence, eds., *Focus on Leadership: Servant Leadership for the 21st Century*, 3rd ed. (Wiley, 2001).

22. Sweet, *Summoned to Lead*, 180.

to teach us semiotics—the art of reading signs—and it worked far better than a classroom discussion would have. That was leadership.

Followers as Leaders

And this is the first of several critiques or applications I wish to make here regarding Sweet's principles of leadership, as summarized briefly on the preceding pages: We do need leadership. And the person warning us against it actually exercises significant leadership. This book is itself evidence of that. We might even call his leadership "charismatic" to some degree. Leonard Sweet is a gifted communicator, both verbally and in writing, and he cultivates a public persona that calls attention not only to his words but also to his person. By his own definitions and warnings, his leadership, his charisma, his competence would be wrong. But I think not.

I think not in part because I trust Leonard Sweet when he says that it is not about him; he persistently and passionately points his audience past himself to the one whom he loves most. When he spoke at my home church, he closed the message, as I imagine he has done in many other settings, with a song: "You can have all this world, but give me Jesus." Sweet is a Jesus freak. By emphasizing his own identity as a follower, he is promoting Jesus' identity as the leader. "He must become greater; I must become less" (John 3:30).

But Jesus gave his disciples a leadership role at the end of his ministry, even if he did not call it that or imagine it in quite the same way that our culture does. I find refreshing the way the twelve apostles shared leadership in that early Jerusalem Church, acting decisively but humbly and collaboratively in addressing the challenges of the earliest church. So I am not fully persuaded that "you and I are never leaders, only followers." I suspect that we are both—sometimes summoned to followership, as Peter was one day by the Sea of Galilee, and sometimes summoned to leadership, as Peter was later on the Day of Pentecost. Where Sweet is right is that we need to be more—much more!—intentional about the leadership we are seeking . . . or delivering. Is it leadership that seeks power at the center or that eschews the trappings and temptations of power in order to seek a greater goal? Is it leadership that plans for control or that prepares for whatever the Spirit creates? Is it leadership that holds onto position or that cheerfully follows when the summons comes to another? Jesus showed us what intentional leadership looks like, and it is not idolatrous to simultaneously follow him and lead others. Did not the Apostle Paul attempt to do the same thing?[23]

Pastors as Leaders

One fairly obvious implication of Sweet's critique of the dominant models and assumptions of leadership is that we also need to reimagine the American cultural model of the pastorate, which is, my own opinion, neither biblical nor healthy. While I would argue that the New Testament did not prescribe a one-size-fits-all model or structure for leadership of the church—thus making irrelevant those Reformation-era squabbles about whether episcopal, presbyterian, or congregational authority was what God intended—it seems clear that the American understanding of church leadership was neither imagined nor condoned by the biblical writers. A "pastor" is a shepherd, not a CEO. Evangelical Protestants are sometimes more Catholic than the papacy in our building of pyramids of power, in our insistence on the compliance of our congregations, and in our bestowing of titles upon ourselves. In contrast, Jesus said, "But you are not to be called 'Rabbi,' for you have one Teacher, and you are all brothers" (Matt 23:8).

Jesus was rather clear on the rest of this too. "You know that those who are regarded as rulers of the Gentiles lord it over them, and their high officials exercise authority over them. Not so with you. Instead, whoever wants to become great among you must be your servant, and whoever wants to be first must be slave of all" (Mark 10:42–44). This is not just an admonition to servant leadership; it is a radical reorientation to life in the kingdom of God. The kingdom is a collective, collaborative effort. The Spirit is given to the church, not just its leaders. The vision bubbles up from the divine imagination of the people of God, not cast downward from those on the mountain. This may involve the five-fold APEPT model (apostle, prophet, evangelist, pastor, and teacher) mentioned in the Epistle to the Ephesians, or other experiments being attempted in churches (such as my own) in which the "pyramid" that represents power relationships in most organizations is either turned on its side or abandoned altogether. But however it looks, it needs to smell like the Spirit.

This is an area in which I wish Sweet would provide a bit more guidance. What, specifically, does he suggest that church leaders do with his

---

23. "Join together in following my example, brothers and sisters, and just as you have us as a model, keep your eyes on those who live as we do" (Phil 3:17).

ideas if they find themselves trapped in a denominational or historical model that does not permit radical revision? How does one transition from the norm to the radical when one is dependent upon the rewards of the traditional structures to even feed oneself, much less to have the opportunity to do significant ministry? This is not a theoretical question for the average pastor, who may find him or herself in the mushy position of relative powerlessness to change structures and practices, but is nonetheless held responsible for the health or growth of the congregation. As responsibilities increase or technology changes, many pastors find themselves struggling to keep up with new or expanding cultural expectations but are afraid to let down their guard, less they find themselves replaced by a younger, more dynamic leader who is able to master the expectations of the moment. How does one move from mush to missional?

Women as Leaders

One answer to the question of how to inculcate shared leadership in the church is to invite more women into leadership roles. It can redeem some of the harm done by patriarchal leadership practices of the past as well as broaden the array of approaches brought to an organization or community, due to the different socializations of men and women. I am not trying here to outright dismiss those who genuinely think, with what they believe is a biblical rationale, that women should not be in senior leadership. My personal experience, however, is that this position is seldom critically examined and has, indeed, become cover for maintaining a status quo that is harmful to men and women alike. More than any shades of complementarianism, however, is the missed opportunity for something marvelously prophetic and redemptive in the sight of a broken world.

Inviting more women into leadership matters then, not merely because of some social agenda, but because of the work of restoration God is doing in the world. If the kingdom of God means anything, it means that all that was broken by the fall is being restored, including the relationship between the sexes. The Western church has so overly sexualized male/female relationships that we are often more proud of our rules in keeping men and women apart than we are in the redemptive progress in bringing them together in mutual honor and respect. We are still so afraid of each other, and this fear causes us to miss many marvelous opportunities to lead and follow together, which seems to have been God's original intent in the garden. But this will require greater sensitivity on the part of men especially, as we have had the power for so very long and have exercised it in ways that have not always been edifying. The women in our churches and other organizations need to find us trustworthy with power before they are willing to serve, much less lead, alongside us.

I respect Leonard Sweet for honoring female church leaders, beginning with his own mother, a Pilgrim Holiness minister. His books utilize both male and female figures as illustrations and as sources of quotations and he appears to be supportive of women leading with strength and wisdom.[24] He avoids gendered language in his books on leadership and advocates for the perspective of women (and others historically excluded) to be included in decision-making: "In a leadership context, 'simultaneity' means bringing people to the table who see things from a variety of perspectives: as women, as ethnic minorities, as the poor, even as the white males from whom we so often hear . . . The goal is to learn to see things from many perspectives simultaneously by listening to one another. This kind of collaboration is sorely lacking in the church."[25] Yes, indeed. And it is past time for that to change.

Educators as Leaders

A final application I suggest here is that we need Christian higher education that challenges and subverts the dominant cultural model, rather than reinforcing or sanctifying it. This should be reflected not only in the content of the classroom but also, and perhaps more significantly, in how the schools themselves are led. Educational institutions are perhaps the most conservative entities in our culture; they still preserve medieval traditions in the twenty-first century and are very slow to change, as countless rueful administrators have discovered. Part of the difficulty is a built-in tension between administration and faculty, which still functions in many respects as a late medieval trade guild, protective of its privileges and of an authority held somewhat independently of administrative decisions. Where else in

---

24. I am curious, however, why he repeatedly insists that Lazarus was Jesus' best friend, when Lazarus has no recorded dialogue with Jesus. Mary and Martha seem to be better friends, and Mary is even willing to subvert patriarchal culture by sitting with the men to listen to Jesus. In fact, the male disciples of Jesus are so often clueless when the women in his life get it. Maybe, in order to achieve the kind of restoration called for here, we need to first re-frame Jesus' own relationships with women, and then follow suit.

25. Sweet, *Summoned to Lead*, 90–91.

American society can one be nearly guaranteed employment for life? And what other role is so influential in cultivating the minds and hearts of our culture's leaders?

Leonard Sweet has spent most of his career in Christian academia, as both administrator and faculty member. He was the president of one seminary, the dean of another, and on the faculty of three. To my knowledge, however, he has not explicitly addressed theological education in specific or higher education in general in his leadership critiques. Perhaps he should. The Christian academy needs to reexamine some of its assumptions about how schools govern themselves without uncritically adopting the patterns of the wider culture. We have sought so hard for respectability that we have lost our distinctiveness in this matter. We claim to be biblical but engage in the same power struggles, create the same inadequate leadership structures, compete with one another with the same ruthlessness, and operate with the same assumptions as do schools where Jesus is neither known nor followed.

My own career path is vaguely similar: I have been faculty, dean, and president in Christian higher education institutions, and I am persuaded that we can do better, that we dare not proclaim the name of Jesus if we are not willing to follow him into the more difficult challenges of life in this broken world, including how we organize ourselves to teach and learn. Perhaps we should also reflect more deeply on what it is to teach or learn, in recognition that our methodologies reflect an uncritical commitment to an industrial/factory model of education, in which raw materials (students) are refined by a manufacturing process into finished products who possess knowledge and skills for vocational service. It is time for the people of God to think more creatively on such matters, and I suspect that Leonard Sweet has more to say to us in this regard. This time we summon him to leadership. Where should Christian higher education go? How can get it there? In what direction is the Spirit blowing in this generation?

The Summoner's Tale

One of the earthier of Geoffrey Chaucer's *Canterbury Tales* is that of the Summoner. In late medieval England this was a person who summoned people to court for their sins and crimes. It was a low level bureaucratic position that was neither terribly popular nor respected. Chaucer uses the marginal nature of this role to powerfully critique a class of religious leaders who were guilty in his day of gross hypocrisy, worldliness, greed, and sloth: the friars. Ironically, the role of the friar had begun only about a century and a half before with the rise of the mendicant (begging) orders, such as the Franciscans, that emphasized poverty and service to the poor. The corruption of the friars in such a relatively short time period is one of the great disappointments of a wonderful reform movement, and a caution to all reformers who come after. They were corrupted by their own success; their reputation for holiness elicited gifts from those who sought a vicarious piety through them, and the unanticipated accumulation of wealth attracted many to their membership who were not prepared to embrace poverty. Through the convenient literary device of putting stories in the mouths of fictional characters, Chaucer is one of the few of his generation brave enough to call attention to this moral decline. The friar of the Summoner's Tale is money-hungry, duplicitous, verbose, and manipulative, and the Summoner embarrasses him, and the friar in his company on the pilgrimage to Canterbury, with a comeuppance that includes an embarrassing plethora of puns on farting.

Leonard Sweet has become our own Summoner, and has told us a gentler, nobler tale, but one with the same warning. We who presume to lead can forget our original calling; we can lose sight of our raison d'etre. So we are summoned to follow first, and until we have learned what followership entails, until we have taken up our cross and walked behind our master to the place of dying, until we have suffered with and for others, until we have felt our own pain so deeply that it has redeemed and restored us, until we are safe to be trusted with power, we are not yet ready to be called "leader" of the people of God. But when the Spirit one day summons us to the task and invites us into the journey, no matter how daunting or awe-inspiring, let us respond like Shackleton—with deep courage and great creativity.

We are then participating in the Great Adventure.

We are then dancing to the great music of the universe.

We are following the Leader of us all.

Bibliography

Cooperrider, David L., and Diana Whitney. *Appreciative Inquiry: A Positive Revolution in Change*. San Francisco: Berrett-Koehler, 2005.

Eliason, Todd. "A Life of Leadership and Influence." *Success*, March 2, 2009. http://www.success.com/article/a-life-of-leadership-and-inspiration.

Kotter, John. *Leading Change*. Cambridge: Harvard University Press, 1996.

MacIntyre, Alasdair. *After Virtue: A Study in Moral Theory*. 3rd ed. South Bend: University of Notre Dame Press, 2007.

Smith, Gordon T. *Courage and Calling: Embracing Your God-Given Potential*. Downers Grove: InterVarsity, 1999.

Sweet, Leonard. *I Am a Follower: The Way, Truth, and Life of Following Jesus*. Nashville: Nelson, 2012.

———. *Nudge: Awakening Each Other to the God Who's Already There*. Elgin, IL: Cook, 2010.

———. *Summoned to Lead*. Grand Rapids: Zondervan, 2004.

2

Wake Up and Smell the Future
From Post-Christian to Post-Church

Jason Clark, PhD (candidate), DMin

> The era of Christendom is over. Postmodern culture is sometimes described as "post-Christian." What captures the post-modern imagination and inflames its spirit is not Christianity. Does the Christian church have any good news left?
>
> —Leonard Sweet[1]

WHY ARE THERE so few Christians in the UK, and why do so many of those who call themselves Christians want nothing to do with church?

Those were questions I found myself struggling with back in the summer of 1999. My wife and I had planted a church in April 1997 on the southwest edge of London. I was working in finance in London, with three small children, whilst we sought to grow a church. Our church plant had grown enough by then that I was about to hand in my notice at work and become a full time pastor. But I was struggling greatly.

I realized that I had been trained in *how* to develop a growing church, but was completely unprepared for the *why* of church—what is the church for in my context. It was only after planting a church that I realised only about 2 percent of people where I lived were actively involved with church,

---

1. Sweet, *SoulTsunami*, 45.

and one of the fastest growing groups around me were Christians who had given up on church completely.

I had been prepared for what do when Christians were looking for a church. I had not been prepared for planting a church in a context where most people wanted nothing to do with Christianity, let alone church. I was completely unprepared for the malaise of Christians who had abandoned church altogether.

So as I faced those questions I sought people and resources to help me understand what was happening. What had led to this context I found myself in, and what did it mean for my church planting and ministry? I came across a paper written by Todd Hunter and Geoff Bailey, a report for the leaders of my denomination (Vineyard Churches) in the United States. It was and still is an insightful paper that explores the cultural changes that were taking place at that time. That paper contained a bibliography listing the key resources that had shaped the content of the paper. I set about working through those resources one by one, until eventually I encountered my first Len Sweet book, *SoulTsunami*.

I remember *SoulTsunami* arriving from Amazon. It was a monster of a book in so many ways. First, it is huge, with a heft and weight you won't notice if you read the Kindle version. Then as I opened it and began to read it, I found that it was rich and complex. I had to read it in small chunks, going away to digest it over a few weeks. To be honest, it was a daunting text, not just for the breadth of its arguments but for the challenges it revealed for my ministry context.

SoulTsunami begins with the suggestion that a tidal wave of change has taken place. We can whine about that change, run away from it, or like Noah facing the flood make new structures to engage with it.[2] Also we can either submerge into our culture, or try to float above it, two methods the church often uses to deal with cultural change. Or again like Noah, we can build boats to be in but not of that cultural change.[3]

Len Sweet wants his readers, readers like me, to "wake up and smell the future."[4] As I read his diagnosis of that tidal wave of change, of the enormity of what was happening around me, I remember thinking how much I wanted to run away and let someone else figure things out. Suddenly, behind my questions I could see that tidal wave of change, and that I had

2. Sweet, *SoulTsunami*, 16.
3. Ibid., 18–23.
4. Ibid., 16.

to make a decision. Would I wake up and navigate that change, or would I run away? I resolved to wake up and face head on what was happening. I found that *SoulTsunami* gave voice to so much of what I was experiencing, it mapped and made sense of what I was struggling to put into words. The book started to help me see the forest for the trees of my own context and culture. My reading of *SoulTsunami* led me to read more of Len Sweet's work and eventually to complete a doctor of ministry degree with him at George Fox Seminary. That program was itself an example of "boat building" as it embraced what was at the time, in 2002, innovative online hybrid learning with face-to-face experiences.

That calling from Len Sweet, to build boats to navigate the tidal wave of change continues to influence my life and ministry. I find myself still leading and navigating the church that I planted back in 1997. The pace of change seems, if anything, to have accelerated since then. In my boat building, I am often overwhelmed by the ongoing challenges of cultural change, but I am still impelled forward by that call from Len Sweet to "wake up and smell the future."

For the rest of this chapter I will share some insights from *SoulTsunami*, which explain the nature of that tidal wave of change. In particular I will highlight the issue of the "post-Christian" that is so apt for the UK with the vestiges of Christianity that survive here. It is this "post-Christian" exploration that has led to my own ongoing study and reflections of the "post-church"; the emergence of a form of Christianity that believes that church is unnecessary. I'll suggest that this "post-church" is not the future of the church at all, but is the kind of submerging into culture that Len Sweet warns us about.

A Tidal Wave of Change

> As a church leader, I am living through an era of institutional decline and degradation some are calling the "Second Great Depression." As a historian of American religion and culture, I am privileged to live in one of the greatest spiritual awakenings in American history, a time some are calling America's "Fifth Great Awakening." What irony that in the midst of a spiritual heatwave in the culture, in the church it's a deep freeze.[5]

---

5. Sweet, *SoulTsunami*, 148.

Len Sweet maps out the decline in organized religion in the West, in particular within Christianity. This decline correlates with a similar decline in how people relate to all organizations and institutions. Yet alongside that decline, there has been a resurgent interest in religion itself that Len Sweet draws our attention to: "Religion is returning to public life. It is once again exercising its political voice. Just when secularization theory seemed to have won, all of a sudden religion gets deprivatized and rediscovers civic responsibility."[6]

The church of modernity, the *Christendom* church has been left behind in a culture that is passing away in a tidal wave of change. A *churched* culture, where church as part of the background to daily life for most people, is over.[7] Yet at the same time there is an upswell of interest in religion by many of those same people.

As an Englishman, it was refreshing to read Sweet's work and see his nuance and awareness of the world outside the United States.[8] Len Sweet is very aware that the passing of Christendom has been far more pronounced in the UK than the United States.

Sweet's writing helped me see what should have been blindingly obvious—the decline of Christianity in the UK. Official statistics show only 9 percent of people in the UK having any connection to a Christian church. There are large variations in the statistic across regions of the UK, and as with all statistics it includes those with the most nominal connection to church—i.e., just Christmas and Easter contact. So I conducted my own review of where I live, an area of SW London with around one hundred and seventy-five thousand people. I estimated local church involvement at a figure of 1–2 percent of that local population. It seemed that Len Sweet was right; the church in the UK is long dead as a background to daily life and experience.

But I was soon to discover one of the fastest growing groups of Christians in the UK; Christians who have given up on church completely, and see no need for being part of any church. This is the *post-church* phenomenon that grows out of the post-Christian that Len Sweet has observed. I now use some more of Len Sweets work to help us understand how the *post-church* emerges from our post-Christian context.

---

6. Ibid., 156.
7. Ibid., 50.
8. Like the important fact that we consume curry in the UK as our most eaten takeaway/takeout (ibid., 371).

Len Sweet offers some "de-" words that map the forces behind the tidal wave of change we are experiencing. This is the rapid change has left much of the church high and dry, living out the cultural realties of a previous Christendom era. At the same time, that church has been missing out on the new interest in religion. The multiple forces of change are de-construction, de-materialization, de-centralization, de-conversion, de-alignment, de-moralization, de-mocratization, de-privatization, de-differentiation, and de-massification.[9] These are some of the *de-forming* forces of postmodern culture that the church must now navigate. They are the new missional context we must engage with as the church of Jesus Christ. Yet they also afford some of the greatest potential of a response cultural change by the church. "Before there can be a Postmodern Reformation, however, there must first be a Postmodern Deformation. Structural deformation leads to spiritual formation, which leads to ecclesial reformation."[10]

In what follows I want to highlight just two of these key de-forming forces and show how they are key to understanding this emergence of the *post-church*.

De-construction

Sweet rightly points out that de-construction is not just a French philosophical movement regarding literary theory and meaning, but it also concerns "moral philosophy." By that he means ethics. There is no neutral place to stand and "observe" life, for we are all participants living life with an ethic. The only issue is what kind of ethic are we already living? De-construction is in part about calling into question and revealing those ethics we are already living.

Stanley Hauerwas has a related well-known axiom: "The church does not have a social ethic; the church is a social ethic."[11] There has been a lie that is now revealed. We cannot just live our lives privately, whilst the realm of ethics is relegated to a separate and optional consideration for Christians. All too often Christians live in their private bubbles, with God as a resource to get through life, unaware of the commitments they are already living out in the cultures around them.

---

9. Sweet, *SoulTsunami*, 149–57.
10. Ibid., 146–47.
11. Hauerwas, *Peaceable Kingdom*, 99.

In the third century AD, Cyprian of Carthage wrote, "Outside the church there is no salvation."[12] Cyprian could have no idea that today his conviction and dictum would be transformed into a new perverted form, the new mantra of "inside the church there is no salvation."

Similar to Hauerwas, Cyprian had in mind that the church was "a distinctive social body with an alternative set of behaviors, disciplines, practices, and social patterns that incorporate believers into a new world."[13]

Yet the church moved away from this self-understanding and became an "imperially allied institution bearing an already attained perfection and thereby the guarantor of salvation for those who belong to it."[14] Those Protestants and then Evangelicals reacting against this control of salvation by the church, developed understandings of the church where the church became merely a vehicle to support the processes of salvation. Salvation became something *non-ecclesial*, and the value of church became how helpful it was in dispensing religious goods and services, to aid people with their private salvation. Jesus is ultimately made into a private saviour, who is accessed through giving intellectual assent to a correct set of beliefs.

There has been a great awareness of that reduction and instrumentalising of the gospel by many evangelicals since the publication of *SoulTsunami*. But instead of leaning back into the past (e.g., to understand Cyprian), to move into the future as Sweet often counsels, many evangelicals have merely continued this instrumentalising process to its logical next stage. Instead of leaning back and understanding salvation and the church as God making "a distinctive social body with an alternative set of behaviors, disciplines, practices, and social patterns that incorporate believers into a new world", many have now have created a "churchless" Christianity.

For it is a very short step from "using" the church to realize some private benefits of salvation, to viewing the church as unnecessary, if not a primary obstacle to the process of salvation. For those making this "churchless" transition in their faith have missed that they are continuing the some of the very problems they have sought to address. Whilst not wanting to be part of a church that is allied to institutional control of salvation they have reduced salvation to something private, with a faith so individualized they are no longer capable of being a distinct social body as the church in society. Also they have reacted to the individualism of modern church

---

12. Cyprian, "To Jubaianus," 272–73.
13. Stone, "Ecclesiality of Mission," 2.
14. Ibid.

worship, the focus on the self that takes up much of church life and worship. Yet instead of forming radical new societies of the body of Christ, they collapsed even further into the logic of individual faith, with a pick and mix choose what I want church life. Len Sweet reminds us there is no *neutral* space for the self-made Christian; instead we all sit in a nexus of complex and deep commitments to ways of life in Western contexts.[15]

We see the post-church malaise manifest in the new Christian confessions and statements that:

"Church doesn't work for me anymore."

"I'm done with church."

"Church just doesn't fit my life anymore."

"Church doesn't meet my needs anymore," etc.

"Does anyone ask whether the church is delivering what the market needs? Imagine if people were encouraged to do their spiritual banking in ways that fit their lifestyle."[16]

Church often becomes a place to stop and visit when we need some extra resources to get through the life we are making for ourselves elsewhere.

Can Christianity be reduced to being measured on how it delivers market needs? What is really at stake is our inability to question the ethics of our lifestyles, and to understand the church as a counter-lifestyle and way of life. Salvation is certainly not something for the church to own and dispense to others, just as it is equally not something for individuals to possess and use for their own lifestyles. Instead, salvation is "a distinct form of social existence. To be saved is literally to be made part of a new people and a new social body—the body of Christ."[17] Salvation is not a guarantee of a way of life for individual consumer dreams, rather it is a way of life and existence with God's people in the world, bringing a new way of living to the world.

---

15. Sweet, *SoulTsunami*, 149–57.
16. Burke, "Out of Ur."
17. Stone, "Ecclesiality of Mission," 3.

De-materialization

Len Sweet also outlines how within modernity the desire to control the material world, led to the undermining of the spiritual.[18] The modern church approach to and for ministry in this controlling environment has often been "got a problem, get a program."[19] By contrast, Sweet maintains that the postmodernworld is about the post-material where "everything solid is melting into thin air."[20] Yet human beings continue to need physical connection. Sweet highlights this with an example of some of the ways people are modifying their bodies to deny and affirm their physicality in this new post material world. This post-material world has formed much of my own on-going research.

This melting away of the material is what Frederick Jameson describes as the "melting of solidity," which Marx foresaw as an outcome of capitalism.[21] This approach to life in Western capitalism is so obvious to most of us that we do not see it anymore. The desire to live comfortable, to own a great home, to have an abundance of amazing relationships, to retire early and live somewhere like on holiday, is the dream most Western people pursue. This is an example of what Charles Taylor calls a "social imaginary."[22] Christians in their worship, their prayers and stories often live out consumer dreams. Those dreams places us at the centre of life, and demands that God provide us all of those things, or else he is deemed to have failed us. Church as we have already mentioned, is all too often a means to support these goals. It is not wrong for God to bless us materially, but we should question of the vision of the gospel for our lives is merely this consumer dream.

Just look at what we share publicly with friends and strangers with ease. Stories of our latest holiday and dream homes we are moving to. We live increasingly isolated lives as we are placed at the centre of them. The decisions we make for are continually made around getting maximum returns for our consumer dreams. We all too often ask, *How will this benefit and advance my agenda?* Once we lived in a world where beliefs held believers, we now live in a world where believers hold beliefs, picking and mixing

---

18. Sweet, *SoulTsunami*, 151.
19. Ibid., 152.
20. Ibid.,151.
21. Smith, *Cultural Transformation*, 3.
22. See Taylor, *Modern Social Imaginaries*.

what they can use to get what they want.[23] "People no longer hunger for salvation or an era of justice, but for 'the feeling, the momentary illusion, of personal well-being, health, and psychic security.'"[24] Christianity has all too often been reduced to a coping mechanism to deal with the disappointments of life.

One thing remains constant for human beings, the way we live and order life is primarily about worship. What we worship, whom we worship and how we worship expresses and makes the lives we live. For worship is the orientation of our time, energy and money into what we think life is about—the "worthship" of life. The only question is what are we worshipping?

Worship becomes primarily about how we organize the basic commitments of life, time, energy and money. Christianity does have an approach to life in the material world and these domains. It is one in which our savior died on a cross on a city refuse heap, and rose from the dead. There is a post-material nature to the Christian faith, the ability to see our place in life, through that experience of Christ on the cross. Instead of consumer dreams our imaginations are invited to be ones of redemption—the cross and God's kingdom. To be a Christian is to imagine how we might bring the kingdom into the refuse sites of life. Instead of Christianity being a dream for escape into a consumer fantasy, it is a call to live out dreams of the kingdom of what Jesus is doing in the places we already live in.

Jeremiah 29 provides a scriptural example of this post-material dream, a social imaginary, and a way to imagine life as part of God's people. It also provides an example of that that looks like in everyday life. All too often Christians jump to verse 11 of Jeremiah 29: "'For I know the plans I have for you,' declares the LORD, 'plans to prosper you and not to harm you, plans to give you hope and a future'" (NIV). We are all too quick to claim this verse for consumer dreams, imagining how God will bless us with wealth and the good life. Yet Jeremiah 29 focuses on a way of life, the ethics of God's economy that subverts the consumer dream. For the promise of Jeremiah 29:11 is predicated on the verses that precede it. God's people who were living within exile, amongst a world of people who don't know God, are invited to live in a particular way. Caught up in a tidal wave of cultural change, they are not allowed to escape, and opt out of the society they find themselves in. That is the very thing Jeremiah condemns in chapter 28. Yet

---

23. Miller, *Consuming Religion*, 90.
24. Ibid., 85.

God's people are not called to just give in and live like everyone else. Instead they are called to we might understand how they are called to build boats like Noah, to be in the world they find themselves in but not of it.

How is that navigation to be made according to Jeremiah? Verses 5–9, carry the call to invest the most important aspects of life: jobs, homes, and relationships, and all the dreams and aspirations we have for them, for the welfare of the city—i.e., those around us. God's people in exile are called to pour themselves into the world, but not for their dreams, but for God's dreams for his world. In a consumer society, who on earth takes their home, jobs and relationships and gives them to God for the welfare of others? No wonder we need the promise of verse 11! God knows that whilst the rest of the Western world is obsessed with their dreams for their own job, homes and relationships, those who give those dreams and realities over for the sake of God and others, need to hear a promise; that God will bless and not harm them.

Imagine what it would do to our Western world, if instead of Christians obsessively praying for great jobs, and moving to dream destinations, if they invested their dreams for the lives of others? Imagine the impact on those living in fear of missing the good life, endlessly tired from the commitments to make a consumer life, if they saw a people able to live fully in this world, free from the self-obsessions of consumer dreams.

The church would be the place where God's people retell the dream of Jeremiah 29, reminding each other that despite the pressures of consumer life, they live in a different reality. It would be a place to connect with each other, to share the struggles and joys of investing life for the welfare of others, centred on the worship of God by his people. It wouldn't be a pick and mix, download on demand spirituality, but a very solid boat riding the waves of life in a post-material world with others.

Hydroponic Ecclesiology

Hydroponics is a method of growing plants without soil. Much of the post-church forms of church can be understood as being like hydroponic plants, rooted in nothing but the air and culture around them. Christians who have become so disillusioned with church that they think they don't need the soil of a church community to nurture them. They think they can float above church spraying their roots with nutrients they want when they need them.

But the reality is that there is no neutral free-floating space to live in. We are all rooted in something, coming from somewhere, owing something to someone. The de-constructed, de-materialized, de-churched Christianity is like an ark built with the hope that it can hover above the church it navigates, submerged in the culture of the world around it.

The advent of globalized capitalism allowed Wesley to confidently declare that the world was his parish. It was the emergence of a new industrial society that allowed Wesley to be able to make that statement. Commerce and methods of travel made a new world that he could enter into as his parish. Yet that amazing cultural agency, the freedom for expression in capitalism has now often collapsed into a self-serving, self-creating anti-institutionalism. Much of what masquerades as being authentic, progressive, expressive, experiential and real, is fuelled by an anti-institutional imagination. The freedom to choose that once allowed Christians to collaborate together for the gospel, now allows Christians to choose a life isolated from others around consumer dreams, instead of a people living for and serving their God together. Or as Jamie Smith puts it:

> Jesus calls us not only to ensure our own salvation in some privatized religious ghetto; he calls us to seek the welfare of the city and its inhabitants all around us. We love God by loving our neighbours; we glorify God by caring for the poor; we exhibit the goodness of God by promoting the common good.
>
> But here's the thing: if you're really passionate about fostering the common good, then you should resist anti-institutionalism. Because institutions are ways to love our neighbours. Institutions are durable, concrete structures that—when functioning well—cultivate all of creation's potential toward what God desires: *shalom*, peace, goodness, justice, flourishing, delight. Institutions are the way we get a handle on concrete realities and address different aspects of creaturely existence. Institutions will sometimes be scaffolds to support the weak; sometimes they function as fences to protect the vulnerable; in other cases, institutions are the springboards that enable us to pursue new innovation. Even though they can become corrupt and stand in need of reform, institutions themselves are not the enemy.[25]

The issue isn't whether you are part of an institution, but what is your imagination for the institutions you are part of? An institution of one, with a life made around you is the consumer dream. For Christians a life

25. Smith, "We Believe."

imagined around Jesus with his people for the sake of the world, is the only place to dream and invest our lives. It is the boat we desperately need Christians to build with others to navigate our emerging globalized world and culture. Or as Len Sweet has put it, will Christians wake up and smell the future, one in which they make their dreams for life, the kingdom of God, with his people? A future in which men and women of God lay down their right for self fulfillment, and find their fulfillment in investing their lives with Christ, with others, for the sake of the world.

Conclusion

Back in my local church, that I planted and pastored, how does this take shape day to day? We are a worshipping community, one that gathers together regularly, not to escape the world, but to worship God as his people, to remind ourselves that we are his people in the world.

Our worship seeks to retell the story of the life, death and resurrection of Jesus. So that story might fund our imaginations and set the priorities for the investments we make in our daily lives. We try to understand how our decisions and acts of daily living are our acts of worship. In that we hope that those around us see the life, death and resurrection of Jesus retold and made real around them. We also hope that people look at us and see a group of people who have a life in common; distinct and alternative to how they are living and one they know they are invited into with us.

Bibliography

Burke, Spencer. "Out of Ur." May 2006. http://www.outofur.com/archives/2006/05/spencer_burke_o.html. Website no longer available.
Cyprian of Carthage. "To Jubaianus, concerning the Baptism of Heretics." In *The Ante-Nicene Fathers*, edited by Alexander Roberts et al., 8:272–73. Grand Rapids: Eerdmans, 1931.
Hauerwas, Stanley. *The Peaceable Kingdom: A Primer in Christian Ethics*. Notre Dame: University of Notre Dame Press, 1991.
Miller, Vincent J. *Consuming Religion: Christian Faith and Practice in a Consumer Culture*. London: Bloomsbury Academic, 2005.
Smith, James K. A. Preface to *Cultural Transformation and Religious Practice*, by Graham Ward. Cambridge: Cambridge University Press, 2005.
———. "We Believe in Institutions." Editorial. *Comment* (magazine), fall 2013. http://www.cardus.ca/comment/article/4039/editorial-we-believe-in-institutions.

Stone, Bryan. "The Ecclesiality of Mission in the Context of Empire." In *Walk Humbly with the Lord: Church and Mission Engaging Plurality*, edited by Viggo Mortensen and Andreas Nielsen, 105–12. Grand Rapids: Eerdmans, 2010.

Sweet, Leonard I. *SoulTsunami: Sink or Swim in New Millennium Culture*. Grand Rapids: Zondervan, 1999.

Taylor, Charles. *Modern Social Imaginaries*. Durham: Duke University Press, 2004.

Ward, Graham. *Cultural Transformation and Religious Practice*. Cambridge: Cambridge University Press, 2005.

3

Preaching as Bricolage

Charles J. Conniry Jr., PhD

WHEN JESUS POINTED OUT that wise teachers in the kingdom of heaven are like homeowners that bring from their storerooms "new gems of truth as well as old" (Matt 13:52 NLT), he was making, among other things, an important observation about the creative task proper to every homiletical undertaking. Good preachers are, to borrow from Claude Lévi-Strauss, *bricoleurs*.[1]

Strauss observed that there is no English equivalent for (the French) bricoleur. A deft bricoleur is one who undertakes odd jobs—a Jack or Jill of all trades, as it were:

> The "bricoleur" is adept at performing a large number of diverse tasks; but, unlike the engineer, he [or she] does not subordinate each of them to the availability of raw materials and tools conceived and produced for the purpose of the project. His [or her] universe of instruments is closed and the rules of his [or her] game are always to make due with "whatever is at hand."[2]

For Strauss there is a sharp difference between an engineer and a bricoleur. The former's tools and materials all have a prescribed purpose and place, and each one has a singular determinate use. The bricoleur's materials, on the other hand, have no predetermined use. Their application is guided solely by the emergence of a set of circumstances that call forth a specific use for that place and time. The key mark of every good bricoleur,

---

1 Lévi-Strauss, *Savage Mind*, 16–36.
2 Ibid., 17.

then, is the skill to use "whatever is at hand" to fashion a certain thing, a *bricolage*, which ably fits its particular application.

Remember MacGyver?

MacGyver, the TV character played by actor Richard Dean Anderson, portrays the quintessential bricoleur. The *MacGyver* series originally aired for seven seasons on ABC between 1985 and 1992, but the character's ability to use ordinary objects to accomplish extraordinary things has had an enduring impact, inspiring the imaginations of people up to the present time. For example, during the Super Bowl XL broadcast in 2006, Anderson reappeared as the MacGyver character in a MasterCard commercial. In a mere thirty seconds he freed himself from a chair to which he was tied, using a pine-tree air freshener as a knife. He then made a grand escape down a makeshift zip line using a tube sock as the trolley. When he landed he quickly fixed and hotwired a dilapidated truck with a paper clip, ballpoint pen, rubber band, a pair of tweezers, nasal spray, and a turkey baster.

The moral of the story? If you can't escape your doom by using a few dollars' worth of random items, like MacGyver-the-bricoleur, there's always MasterCard®!

Anderson appeared again as MacGyver in fall 2012 when he did several short movies for Mercedes-Benz, which stayed up on the company's website through most of 2013.

People remember good bricoleurs!

Bricolage in Creation and Glory

Bricoleurship reaches all the way back to our primordial Beginning. While theologians argue for *creatio ex nihilo* (creation out of nothing), Genesis portrays a Master Bricoleur: "The Lord God formed *from the ground* all the wild animals and all the birds of the sky" (Gen 2:19, my emphasis). God "formed the man *from the dust of the ground*. He breathed the breath of life into the man's nostrils, and the man became a living person" (2:7, my emphasis). Then God "took out one of the man's ribs and . . . made a woman" (2:21b–22a).

God made us from dirt and breath (*ruach*)!

After our awakening to things good and evil, God made our first set of clothes from animal hide.

God wrote the first words of the covenant with Israel on stone, a readily available material on top of Mt. Sinai . . . and made Moses carve the second set, which is instructive because it illustrates that bricoleuring can be a co-creative phenomenon—something we do *with God.*

While animals like beavers and birds make good use of available materials in the fashioning of dams and nests, bricoleurship in all its creative artistry is a uniquely human phenomenon—a facet of our Divine Image.

God created us to be co-creators.

The story of humanity's love affair with God begins and ends in gardens, but with a notable difference in the features of the story's second garden, which highlights the role that redeemed humanity plays in the fashioning of the new heavens and new earth. Our co-creative activities have in fact been underway since the first garden.

Both Genesis and Revelation describe gardens. While there are similarities between where we begin and where we end up, there are notable differences as well. In Genesis God is the Master Gardner, making each tree beautiful to the eye and its fruit sumptuous to the taste. God planted each one in its proper place and watered his masterpiece with an elaborate irrigation system of rivers. The ancient historian, speaking in the present tense, tells us, "The gold of that land is exceptionally pure; aromatic resin and onyx stone are also found there" (Gen 2:12).

In Revelation the garden is Central Park of New Jerusalem, the city that God and God's people inhabit. Gone is creation's circadian rhythm: moon and sun, night and day, "for the glory of God illuminates the city, and the Lamb is its light" (21:23b). Gone as well is Sabbath, for our salvation rest is perpetual (cf. Heb 4). Gone is the Tree of the Knowledge of Good and Evil along with the potentialities of death and sorrow and crying and pain. "All these things are gone forever" (Rev 21:4). There is no temple. In its place is the city's new temple: the Lord God Almighty and the Lamb (21:22).

Even more telling than what is not there, however, is what the new city and its garden include. New Jerusalem and the garden are replete with artifacts of human making. "All the nations," says John the Revelator, "will bring their glory and honor into the city" (21:26).

What does John mean by "glory and honor"?

Richard Mouw and Andy Crouch both believe that John is talking about the best of human culture—transformed and glorified. "Not all of the items of pagan culture," Mouw writes, "will be gathered, as is, into the Holy City." He continues,

A pagan ship will be changed into a redeemed ship—but it will still be a ship. But other things will have to have their identities, their basic functions, transformed; some of them will be changed almost beyond recognition. Swords will become plowshares. Spears will be changed into pruning hooks. Marxist posters will become aesthetic objects, which will enhance the beauty of the City. Perhaps missiles will become play areas for children.[3]

What this insight means for us in practical terms, says Mouw, is that we "must train ourselves to look at the worlds of commerce and art and recreation and education and technology, and confess that all of this 'filling' belongs to God" and, accordingly, "engage in the difficult business of finding patterns of cultural involvement, which are consistent with that confession." He argues that if God has not given up on human culture, neither should we.[4]

Crouch's playful elaboration on Mouw's thesis is worth quoting at length:

> What cultural goods represent the "glory and honor" of the many cultural traditions we know? . . . My own personal list of "the glory and honor of the nations" would surely include Bach's *B Minor Mass*, Miles Davis's *Kind of Blue* and Arvo Pärt's "Spiegel im Spiegel"; green-tea crème brûlée, fish tacos and bulgogi; *Moby-Dick* and the *Odyssey*; the iPod and the Mini Cooper. Of course I don't expect any of them to appear without being suitably purified and redeemed, any more than I expect my own resurrected body to be just another unimproved version of my present one. But I will be very surprised if they are not carried in by one or another of the representatives of human culture, for they are part of the glorious best that human beings have made of the twelve-tone scale, the flavors of the natural world, language, the microchip and the internal combustion engine. (For the cows' and fishes' sake, I suppose the transformed meals in the new Jerusalem will be vegetarian, but surely they will be a grand improvement on tofurkey.)[5]

We may quibble about the specific artifacts that will make the new city and garden's final cut, but Mouw and Crouch have picked up on the scent of something wonderful.

---

3 Mouw, *When the Kings Come Marching In*, 19–20 (my emphasis).
4 Ibid., 20–21.
5 Crouch, *Culture Making*, 170.

It inspires the imagination to envision the ultimate disposition of God's created order as a glorious combination divine and human artifacts drawn from every generation past, present, and future.

The new heavens and new earth . . . *a bricolage*!

We should not be surprised, therefore, that the genius of divine-human interaction throughout the ages is displayed in the same bricoleuring activities that comprise creation's ultimate state in eternal glory. We are, after all, God's image bearers. God is Master Bricoleur and we are God's co-bricoleurs. We collaborate with God in the making of arks and temples and altars and cathedrals. We use wood and stone and gold and gemstones to create sacred things from materials not sacred in themselves, and in the end, God will transform much of the non-sacred components of human culture into things fit for the new city and its garden. God and human beings joined in mysterious and wondrous co-creation!

A Prophetic and Apostolic Tradition

God's prophets, apostles, and preachers are semiotic bricoleurs who use belts and sticks and stones and fleeces and olive oil and sundials and clay jars and old rags—among a host of other odds and ends—to bring their God-inspired messages to life.

The prophet Jeremiah, for example, leveraged numerous artifacts to make God-inspired points, none of which were gathered with any predetermined use. In Jeremiah 13 God instructed the prophet to purchase a linen belt and wear it for a while. Then Yahweh told Jeremiah to hide it in a crevice in the rocks for a long period of time. Finally, God told him to retrieve it. When Jeremiah did so, he discovered that the belt was useless. Then the word of the Lord came to him:[6]

This is what the Lord says: "In the same way I will ruin the pride of Judah and the great pride of Jerusalem. These wicked people, who refuse to listen to my words, who follow the stubbornness of their hearts and go after other gods to serve and worship them, will be like this be—completely useless!" (Jer 13:9–10).

Several chapters later in the book of Jeremiah God tells the prophet to observe two baskets of figs placed in front of the temple. One basket

---

6 The phrase, "Then the word of the Lord came to me," often signals the divine appropriation of a given artifact in the Bible's prophetic corpus, which was not envisioned (by the prophet at least) until the moment of application.

contains perfectly ripened figs, ready to eat, and the other has poor figs that are unfit to eat. Once Jeremiah makes that observation, the word of the Lord comes to him. God says that the good figs represent those already taken into Babylonian captivity while the second basket reflects how God will treat the treacherous people who still remain in the city. Like the "poor figs, which are so bad they cannot be eaten," says Yahweh, "so I will deal with Zedekiah king of Judah, his officials, and the survivors from Jerusalem . . . I will make them abhorrent and an offense to all the kingdoms of the earth, a reproach and a byword, an object of ridicule and cursing, wherever I banish them" (24:8–9).

A linen belt and two baskets of figs . . . artifacts whose application in each instance is guided by the emergence of a set of circumstances that call forth a specific use for that place and time. The deft use of "illustrative material" is bricoleurship . . .

Bricoleurship is also displayed in the creative blending of intellectual artifacts drawn from different worlds. Think of Paul's inventive juxtaposition in Romans 12:1 of λογικός, a predominately Greek concept from which we derive the word *logic*, and λατρεία, a word used in the Septuagint to describe the sacred duties of the priests, which they carried out every day in the tabernacle and (after its construction) the temple.

Paul brings together two salient concepts, one from Greek philosophy and the other from the Torah . . . and with a stroke of bricoleuring genius uses these concepts to create something new and uniquely Christian. He calls upon us as followers of Jesus to offer our bodies as *living sacrifices* and describes this priestly activity as λογικὴν λατρείαν. Translators have struggled to find the best way to express this odd conceptual mixture from Athens and Jerusalem. The KJV perhaps offers the best rendering, "reasonable service," but its brevity and semantic distance from our day and time require more explanation.

Paul in his use of λατρεία was underscoring *daily sacred service*, which included the morning and evening sacrifices, as well as everything else that priests in God's tabernacle and temple had to do. Priests served as arbiters of disputes, they inspected houses for toxic mold, and had to be present to people's needs. They also had to be ready to dispatch the people's freewill offerings, fellowship offerings, and sin offerings. These sacred duties continued day in and day out, week in and week out, and month in and month out . . . that is λατρεία. Paul in Romans 12 describes us as both the sacrifices (our bodies) and the priests who offer them. And it is something we do on *a daily, moment-by-moment basis*.

Paul uses λογικός to highlight the *manner* by which we render this sacred service. We do this out of a set disposition and purpose of mind. It is *reasoned*, which is to say, *intentional* and *thoughtful*. This daily, moment-by-moment sacred service is achieved by directing our minds and hearts Godward.

How do we put *ourselves* on the altar every day? We do so by mindfully and intentionally offering every thought, every action, and every conversation to God. This as Paul conceives it is our λογικὴν λατρείαν.

We offer our bodies as living sacrifices when we drive our car with appropriate mindfulness. The driver in the lane next to ours shows interest in crossing into our lane . . . in front of us. We notice this . . . even before she puts on her turn indicator. We have a choice. We can depress the accelerator and eliminate the gap, pretending to change the station on the radio to mask our complicity . . . or we convert this moment into an act of worship, dropping back and making plenty of room for our road-mate to enter "our lane." As we do so, we can think of how much God loves that person and offer a prayer for her. Or simply offer a breath prayer: "This, Lord Jesus, I do for you."

Eugene Peterson's *The Message* captures well the meaning of Paul's conceptual bricolage: "Take your everyday, ordinary life—your sleeping, eating, going-to-work, and walking-around life—and place it before God as an offering."

The number of didactic bricolages in Scripture is legion! We would weary ourselves to consider the occurrences of bricolage in the book of Ezekiel alone (his diorama of Jerusalem stands out as one of the Bible's most imaginative bricolages). We delight in Paul's creative appropriation of the Altar to the Unknown God to bring those assembled at the Areopagus into deeper conversation about Jesus and the resurrection. But Jesus, the Master-Bricoleur-Incarnate, stands far above the rest.

Jesus used mud, dirt drawings, and parables with a multitude of artifacts to teach his people. He transformed two elements of the Passover Seder into the symbols of his body and blood, enacting the Eucharist. He adapted those elements in a manner that was appropriate to that particular set of circumstances, creating a wonderful and mysterious convergence of the Passover and the Passion.

But history's ultimate bricolage is nothing other than the cross. Jesus took the most brutal and widely used tool of execution in the ancient world[7] and transformed it into the most cherished and widely recognized symbol of God's love. Crucifixion, as Martin Hengel rightly stated, "was an utterly offensive affair, 'obscene' in the original sense of the word."[8] Before Jesus' death, burial, and resurrection, it would have been inconceivable to believe that the eternally existent Son of God, the one through whom all things were created and in whom all things hold together, would consummate God's redemption of humanity by dying in such a way. Though prophetically anticipated in passages like Psalm 22 and Isaiah 53, no one (except God) could have imagined that the cross, a symbol of torturous death, would ultimately stand as God's signature of life.

A Long Tradition

Faithful preachers and teachers since Pentecost have stood in the great tradition of divine-human bricoleurship, leveraging their skills in proclaiming the message of the cross. "The message of the cross is" as the Apostle Paul notes, "foolish to those who are headed for destruction! But we who are being saved know it is the very power of God" (1 Cor 1:18). Therefore we join the Apostle in saying, "May I never boast about anything except the cross of our Lord Jesus Christ."

Yes, the age of reason spawned its fair share of engineer-like preachers and teachers whose primary aim was to legitimize Christianity's truth claims at the bar of human rationality. Still, the past and present are witness to many artisans of truth, like Justin Martyr, Irenaeus, Augustine of Hippo, Teresa of Avila, George Fox, John Wesley, Charles Spurgeon, Barbara Brown Taylor, Billy Graham, and Leonard Sweet—faithful bricoleurs all, whose brilliance and creativity are adding treasures to the city and garden to come.

A Personal Reflection about My Friend

Len Sweet stands as one of the early twenty-first century's greatest semiotic bricoleurs. I have been blessed by Len's ministry for thirty years. He has

---

7 One of the most incisive treatments of crucifixion in the ancient world is Hengel, *Crucifixion in the Ancient World*, 1977.

8 Ibid., 22.

enriched my thinking and preaching in countless ways. Len is better than anyone I know at gathering available materials—of all shapes and sizes and kinds—and assembling them into masterpiece bricolages. He does this in his writing, teaching, preaching, and life.

I am also honored to know that Len counts me as a friend. We have served together at George Fox Evangelical Seminary for almost two decades. He loves Jesus! And he is winsome, brilliant, and passionately committed to shaping new generations of Jesus-loving bricoleurs. He models what he teaches and preaches, which the following story illustrates.

One time I was sitting with Len in his home office on Orcas Island. I was sharing about my dad and how he always seemed to get into conflict with other drivers when he was behind the wheel. I mused about the fact that road rage seems to have originated in Southern California. "That's probably not a coincidence," I said to Len.

I went on to describe how my father had a special air-horn kit installed in his 1961 Buick Electra 225—*five* air horns with a high-pressure air compressor. It was tuned to sound an F 7th chord . . . like a freight train. The decibel level was equivalent to that of a freight train. When my dad hit the horn, the unsuspecting travelers in the vehicles in front of us would undergo a visible molecular transformation.

My dad eventually traded in the Buick for a Cadillac, but not before transferring the horns to the new car. Eventually he added a PA system to the car so he could supplement the deafening horn blasts with verbal expressions about the other drivers' families of origin.

About that time I noticed Len typing on his laptop. "Catching up on an email"? I asked. "No," he replied, "I'm writing down your story"!

Good bricoleurs always have their eyes and ears open to "whatever is at hand!"

Bibliography

Crouch, Andy. *Culture Making: Recovering our Creative Calling*. Downers Grove: InterVarsity, 2008.

Hengel, Martin. *Crucifixion in the Ancient World and the Folly of the Message of the Cross*. Philadelphia: Fortress, 1977.

Lévi-Strauss, Claude. *The Savage Mind*. Chicago: University of Chicago Press, 1966.

Mouw, Richard. *When the Kings Come Marching In: Isaiah and the New Jerusalem*. Grand Rapids: Eerdmans, 2002.

4

Heretics and the Way Forward

Dottie Escobedo-Frank, DMin

SOME CHURCH LEADERS, DOWN through the ages, have been labeled as "heretics." At times, the term has been received like mud flung in the face of people with good intentions, causing pain, angst, and further separation. Ellis Peters, in *The Heretic's Apprentice*, reimagines it this way: "One century's saint is the next century's heretic . . . and one century's heretic is the next century's saint. It is as well to think long and calmly before affixing either name to any man."[1]

But we are entering an era where change is embraced, sought after, and valued. When systems, economies, and modalities of operation are failing, change becomes the new value. Heretics today could actually be well positioned to pave the path for renewal and the re-forming of the church.

Dr. Leonard Sweet, a change-agent in the field of religious expression and experience, is a leader who both looks to the future and the past simultaneously. His image-logo is a man on a swing, with his body leaning back while his legs reach for the sky. It is a precarious image to live out. Most church leaders are firmly grounded in the past, and are merely taking peeks at the future. But to lean and reach both ways is to be willing to ruffle the church feathers, and to suffer being called names of all kinds. Yes, Sweet and other thoughtful faith leaders have occasionally been referred to as "heretics."

---

1. "Heresy," *Goodreads*.

While the so-called heretic has previously been considered wholly negative, the changing world may just be calling for heretics to lead us forward. This idea is not new, however. G. K. Chesterton, in *Heretics*, says, "The word 'heresy' not only means no longer being wrong: it practically means being clear-headed and courageous. The word 'orthodoxy' not only no longer means being right; it practically means being wrong."[2]

To be a change agent, to refuse to be stuck in "what was" often includes being labeled as "wrong," or at least being misunderstood. Some "heretics" however respond to this by simultaneously saying *Ouch* and *Hallelujah*. To be the recipient of name-calling is often the mark of someone who is pulling us reluctantly forward.

The Jesus Factor

Remember, Jesus' religious community labeled our Lord as a "heretic." We know he refused to cease the actions that often got him in trouble. Jesus healed a man on the Sabbath near the Sheep Gate, at the pool of Bethsaida.[3] (A man who had suffered for thirty-eight years.) Jesus didn't seem to care too much about how others labeled him. He made it possible for a man to walk for the first time in nearly four decades!

But instead of being wholly amazed at the new work of God, the religious leaders were horrified. They asked him why he would heal on the Sabbath, the day of rest. Some even wanted to kill him for his two "unorthodoxies": the decision to heal on the Sabbath and his claim that he was equal to God.

This tension between the religious establishment and the life and teachings of Jesus continued to fester. After Lazarus was raised from the dead, they were so frightened by his power and influence; they began to formally plot his demise.[4]

At Jesus' trial before Pilate, the leaders of his religion claimed he deserved to be crucified because he claimed to be the "King of the Jews."[5] In the end, he died for his faith-forward vision and actions.

Out of Jesus' death and resurrection, a new faith was formed. It was not a faith separate from the mother faith, but a faith that was an extension,

2. Ibid.
3. John 5:1–18.
4. John 11:47–54.
5. John 19:1–16.

a growth, and reached out to a new direction. It was a faith that extended beyond one group of people and offered entrance to the whole world. It lessened, even removed, the importance of many traditional rituals and even some dogmas. Jesus' life and death changed the future of the world, birthed from teaching and a way of life that some described as "heretical."

The Core Belief

Christianity, the "new" faith that began with rapid change, has now morphed into an institution that at its core prefers conformity. The church even began to claim, over the years, which was God's side of a war; who is considered good and who is evil enough to be burned on a stake; and which sins are worse than others. The Mother Church has fought passionately to retain its traditions, no matter how ugly some of them may be, throughout the ages.

Some of us have rules that tell us who can be ordained or not, who can serve Holy Communion or Agape Feast, and how pastors and laity may be permitted work together, all the while retaining many strict boundaries.

We tend to call our center "orthodoxy." Orthodoxy, by definition, means: "Adhering to the accepted or traditional and established faith, especially in religion. Adhering to what is commonly accepted, customary, or traditional: an orthodox view of world affairs."[6]

We tend to rightly think of orthodoxy as pertaining to the central understanding of Jesus Christ as Savior, Son of God, part of the Holy Trinity. We necessarily guard these understandings with our preaching, teaching, and how we filter our interpretation of ideas and current events emerging in the world at large. We stand firm on the basics of our faith.

Leonard Sweet, in responding to his critics and name-callers, stated this view with clarity:

> I hope therefore I have done nothing with this treatise to divide the body in any way, but only to continue to nourish it as is always my aim and task as a Jesus followers [sic] . . .
>
> For I am passionate about the historical creeds of the faith (Apostolic, Nicene, Chalcedon, etc.) and the authority and inspiration of the Scripture. While my roots are Wesleyan, I affirm what the Reformers taught about the centrality of Christ, the glory of God, and the truth of the Scripture. As Augustine put it first, but

---

6. *Free Dictionary*, s.v. "Orthodox."

Wesley made it famous: "In essentials unity, in non-essentials liberty, but in all things love."[7]

When theologians, scholars, and faith leaders are challenged by their work being defined as "heresy," many, of necessity, find a way to reaffirm orthodoxy, in order to allow for new angles and postures in following after Jesus, while retaining a central core. Growth often emerges out of a basis of stability. Therefore many spiritual visionaries and pioneers often first restate their faith in foundational beliefs, before speaking the truth as they see it.

When the core belief is affirmed, it is somewhat easier, though often still difficult, to allow for imagination and expansion in our understanding of God. Since theology is about the study of God, and since we are limited human beings, we can assume that none of us know the depth and breadth and height of the God who is beyond all that we are and all that we know. It takes humility to ground oneself in core beliefs, while allowing for growth into new experiences.

The Former Understanding of Heretical Beliefs

A heretic, however, is "someone who believes or teaches something that goes against accepted or official beliefs. A dissenter from established religious dogma. One who dissents from an accepted belief or doctrine: nonconformist."[8]

This old definition of a heretic is steeped in traditional understandings. The church is a system of homeostasis; a system that always seeks to restore order by bringing things back to the former center. In other words, the church can be an organized system, which seeks to fight off all forms of change. However, the definition of "heretic," as described above, can provide some possibilities of moving away from "official" or "accepted" views, and accepting the challenge of growth. Many valued church leaders have broken away from the norm and in the end, have become the heroes of the future of the church.

Below is a list of a few church leaders who were originally called "heretics" that should give thoughtful people some pause in immediately labeling anything new as automatically unorthodox:

---

7. Sweet, "Response to Recent Misunderstandings," 2007, http://leonardsweet.com/response.

8. *Merriam-Webster*, s.v. "Heretic."

Martin Luther, leader of the Protestant Reformation, who was formally excommunicated from the Catholic Church.

John Wesley, founder of the Methodist movement, who took preaching beyond the boundaries of the walls of the church, and formed a new way that was not sanctioned by the Church of England.

George Fox, the founder of the Society of Friends, who endured eight imprisonments for blasphemy, stirring up an insurrection, and other unorthodoxies.[9]

Heretics are only seen as rebels when their ideas are brand new, but often, over time, many are eventually considered saints and bright lights after their deaths.

Some well-known Christians were so "heretical" that they were laid to rest in the Dissenter's Cemetery, the burial place for nonconformists or those who were no longer connected to the Church of England. These include:

William Blake, poet, and his wife, Catherine

John Owen, Congregational minister

Susanna Wesley, mother of the Methodist movement

Daniel Defoe, author of *Robinson Crusoe*

John Bunyan, author of *The Pilgrim's Progress*

Isaac Watts, hymn writer.[10]

These notorious "rebels" fostered change that was considered unacceptable in their day, and yet today, they are honored as fathers and mothers of "orthodox" movements within the body of Christ. Alan Deutschman, in *Change or Die*, reminds us that "one of the reasons we resist change, unconsciously at least, is that it invalidates years of earlier behavior."[11]

The church, steeped in ritualistic behavior and deep historical memories, has often unwittingly created an organization in which change is seen

---

9. "Life of George Fox," http://www.ushistory.org/penn/fox.htm.

10. "Wesley's Chapel and Museum of Methodism, London," *Sacred Destinations* (website), http://www.sacred-destinations.com/england/london-wesley-chapel.

11. Deutschman, *Change or Die*, 85.

as evil and where homeostasis powerfully numbs out the fresh winds of the Spirit.

George Fox penned this poem, reflecting on the push against change:

> The Papists they cry, Conform.
>
> And the Turk, he cries, Conform.
>
> And did not the heathen Emperors cry, Conform?
>
> And the Presbyterian, he cried, Conform.
>
> And the Independents . . .
>
> So everyone that gets the uppermost, and gets the staff of
>
> authority, commands . . .
>
> But no law of Jesus requires it, who said, "Freely you have received, freely give."[12]

For many visionary leaders of the faith, the sacrifice of change was more than they had imagined. What died in their time was traditionalism and orthodoxy, and what rose was a fresh move of the Holy Spirit. Voltaire, in *The Age of Louis XIV*, summarizes the situation by writing, "It is dangerous to be right in matters on which the established authorities are wrong."[13]

"Dangerous" is the correct word for living a life where ideas are beyond the current understanding or politics of those in power. One must understand, if they are looking to lead the church forward—that this position of leadership is not comfortable, generally accepted, or welcomed. In fact, it will often be disturbingly painful, unacceptable, and quashed. Such people often suffer disconnection from their religion, disowning by their families, imprisonment, and even death. These are the realities of the bold and courageous rebels of Jesus that are sometimes referred to as "heretics."

The New Culture of Valuing "Heretics"

In times where change is essential for survival—heretics, creatives, sarcastics, artists, and irreverents move from the edge to the center. Change requires real change, and heretics can be the creators of much-needed change. Church consultant Gil Rendle states that we need to protect and

---

12. Ibid., 27.
13. "Heresy," www.goodreads.com/quotes/tag/heresy.

value the voices of the creative deviants.[14] Entrepreneur Seth Godin says we need "heretics" writing: "Heretics are the new leaders. The ones who challenge the status quo, who get out in front of their tribes, who create movements. The marketplace now rewards and embraces the heretics. Suddenly, heretics, troublemakers, and change agents aren't merely thorns in our side—they are the keys to our success."[15]

Guides are those who travel out ahead of the group in order to see what lies in the future, who guide the herd to a new path, an unforeseen path. It takes new leaders to point the way forward in a world where the church is seen as irrelevant, unnecessary, and at times, little more than a house of hypocrites.

Sutton confirms that, in order to innovate, we must be willing to support risky projects. He urges us to "support a few crackpots, heretics, and dreamers, especially if they are wildly optimistic about their ideas."[16]

Clay Christensen, a professor from Harvard Business School, created the term "disruptive innovation" to explain "a new category of 'good enough,' low-cost products and services that were under-engineered to meet the basic needs of mass consumers."[17]

While *heretic* is a charged word for church people, in many ways, it's very radical-ness is what offers us hope. When the Mother Church is stuck on a plateau, teetering in decline, or living on life-support, a radical transformation is required. Suddenly sarcastics, irreverents, troublemakers, and rebels on the edges of religious institutions become the transformational agents. Suddenly, those on the outside, or those that have formerly been pushed over the edge, are the very ones who can point to a way out of the mess we've all made together.

In our day, the ones who are being called all sorts of names, like heretic, are often the very ones we need to listen to. The "other" may be the one who starts a new revolution of love for Jesus Christ and for the world he died for. Pastor Rudy Rasmus says, "Revolutions have always come from a groundswell of people who have been marginalized by systems and processes, and have been excluded from the benefits of the institution."[18]

---

14. Rendle, *Journey in the Wilderness*, 100.
15. Godin, *Tribes*, 11.
16. Sutton, *Weird Ideas That Work*, 112.
17. Saul, *Social Innovation, Inc.*, 59.
18. Rasmus, *Jesus Insurgency*, 71.

And so, there is an upside-down-and-turn-around nature to any revolution. Who we may actually need in this strange new day are those who we have pushed out, disempowered, and disenfranchised. We may need pastors without credentials; laity who serve communion in secret because a community needs the Lord's Supper; immigrants who hide out without proper documentation; people who are typically "un-allowed" to be ordained; persons of color or cultural variation; and even young people who may have a more genuine faith than some adults. These are the revolutionaries we need to lean into in order to find our resurgence and make disciples of Jesus Christ in a changing world.

Social Innovation in the Church: A New/Old Idea

Social innovation is being adopted by business in today's world. A business philosophy that seeks to make a difference in the world, while simultaneously making a profit.

Some businesses have caught on to the idea that companies can work to change the world as a part of their strategy for profit. If even the world of the profit margin knows that working for the good of society and caring for the least of these is crucial to being seen as valuable within our culture, certainly the church can reach into its memory bank and it Scriptures to focus on transformation of the world as we rework an old idea in a new world.

An example of this is when CrossRoads United Methodist Church began feeding the homeless. Since the city decided to give us a cease and desist order, calling for the church to shut down its ministry on church property, many people heard about our disagreement with the City of Phoenix via media coverage. We received emails from all over the world, some of which were threatening and bullying. But one very consistent group of emails came from people who called themselves "atheists" and "agnostics." They often made it clear hat they did not believe in God, or in religion, but if they did, CrossRoads would be their home church. The witness to the world, of caring for others who might not be acceptable in society, was powerful even as it was painful for the church. In this way, CrossRoads was both disruptive and transformative.

Another example is the rich tradition of offering a tithe of one's income as a base of support for the mission and ministry of the church. Under this tradition, the members of the church community are financially responsible for the ministry. The expectation being that all members will give 10 percent of their income in order operate the church. But in today's economy we have found that offerings no longer support the ministry as they have in the past. Len Sweet reminds his students that churches need to find other avenues to fund the mission of the church.

CrossRoads United Methodist Church has been growing in the reverse economic direction. We are larger in number, and many of the additional souls have come from the lower economic strata. We rejoice in this trend, because the church needs to become a place of economic diversity, where the poor are assisted, and are even encouraged to join the table of leaders. CrossRoads has a mission to the poor and hungry, but if we relied on offerings alone, we would not be able to finance mission. Consequently, we have extended our funding to include a preschool (relational and caring funding), a steeple with a cell tower (passive and marketing funding), and a farmer's market (community needs funding). These diverse income streams support the mission of feeding people.

This new way of looking at mission funding is contrary to orthodox ideas around church members paying for mission through tithing. It can even rearrange our received theology (understanding of God and relationship to God), biblical mandates, and certainly church tradition. Similar to how Jesus was condemned for healing on the Sabbath, the church that embodies this new way of funding could be seen as heretical and off center, not staying true to "God's plan" of tithing a tenth of one's income.

Admittedly, this is a rather minor change, but even this small change has been regularly questioned, challenged, and has even led to some name-calling.

The Church Is Ripe for Positive Heretics to Lead Us Forward

Recently, when listening to the stories of new pastors fresh out of seminary and serving in their first churches, a clear pattern began to emerge. This new group of clergy was almost entirely made up of people who had grown up in the church. But is that what is needed today?

What the church may need today is pastors and leaders who did not grow up within her four walls. But maybe what we need is artists and creatives and social entrepreneurs and revolutionaries and health professionals and service laborers to lead us forward into a new day in the kingdom?

Our staff just threw a going-away party for the church office manager who had been with us for over two years. We purposefully hired her for her office skills and because she was an outsider. Amy did not grow up in church and did not claim to follow any faith. She had never read the Scriptures, did not know what a bulletin was, and didn't understand our Christianese vocabulary. And so she questioned us relentlessly. We learned what we said that made no sense to the world outside the church. We learned which practices were contrary to an outsider's idea of "love and care." And we learned to read our Scriptures with fresh eyes.

Amy had to look up the scriptures (she *Goggled* them) in order to prepare the bulletin. We would talk about the meaning of the stories so she could choose a picture or art piece for the bulletin. One day, around Advent (a word that had no meaning to her), the sermon title was "Room at the Inn." I asked her if she knew where that title came from and after pondering for a second or two, she replied,

"Is it the name of a bar?"

After laughing and telling her the story she insisted that it definitely would be an excellent name for a bar!

When she first heard the story about Peter denying Jesus, she was angry, saying Peter was on her "Not-So-Good" List (my words: hers were a little more colorful). Throughout our time together, Amy opened my eyes to the words and stories of the Scriptures as she shared with me her initial thoughts about these narratives that she had never heard before. My soul was refreshed in her presence, and the church was revitalized as our systems were questioned, and eventually changed, because one beloved "outsider" lived and led among us.

Amy definitely feels more at home in the realm of heresy than that of orthodoxy. She is not even an insider. But this is the time when the Amys and Len Sweets are needed to pull us to a new future. A future of hope and joy will come, but not before we go through the valley of the shadow of death. On the other side of this valley, lest we forget, is where we find resurrection and life.

Heretics may just be the new visionaries, missionaries, and emissaries. They are the ones who will lead us forward in the ways of the fresh Spirit of Jesus.

Bibliography

Deutschman, Alan. *Change or Die: The Three Keys to Change at Work and in Life.* New York: HarperCollins e-books, 2007.

Godin, Seth. *Tribes: We Need You to Lead Us.* New York: Portfolio, 2008.

Rasmus, Rudy, and Dottie Escobedo-Frank. *Jesus Insurgency: The Church Revolution from the Edge.* Nashville: Abingdon, 2012.

Rendle, Gil. *Journey in the Wilderness.* Nashville: Abingdon, 2010.

Saul, Jason. *Social Innovation, Inc.: 5 Strategies for Driving Business Growth through Social Change.* San Francisco: Jossey-Bass, 2010.

Sutton, Robert I. *Weird Ideas That Work: 11 ½ Practices for Promoting, Managing, and Sustaining Innovation.* New York: Free Press, 2002.

5

What's Going on Here?
Trusting God's Story in Your Own

Dwight J. Friesen, DMin

AT THE FIRST SESSION with Leonard Sweet in my doctoral program, Len made a prediction that turned out to be shockingly accurate. After surveying the faces of the wide-eyed and eager cohort seated in a circle at a Quaker Retreat center outside of Portland, Oregon, he predicted that most of us in the room would experience a vocational redirection during our studies. I didn't believe him. After all, I had recently pioneered a new missional community and I couldn't fathom a change. But, it turns out that Len was right. Within the course of our program, nearly every leader in that room bore a significant change of direction within their life, ministry, or both.

I don't know about you, but my life hasn't turned out the way I envisioned it would. All of my dreaming and scheming has proven to be a living testimony to the proverb that says, "People make plans but God directs their steps."[1] That foresight fails us is a reality that Len has named by often challenging the modern leadership myth of vision. "Vision is overrated,"[2] I remember him saying. Smoke and mirrors, sleight of hand, all allude to the truth that vision is an easily fooled sense.

Len has taught and trained leaders for a long time. Yet in all his years of teaching, there is only one book, other than the Bible, that Len has

---

1. Prov 16:9, my paraphrase.

2. See Sweet, *Summoned to Lead*, for his language around the limitations of the modern notion of vision, while enlarging our imaginations unto attuning ourselves to the voice of God.

assigned to every doctoral cohort he has worked with. And that book was written by a person who epitomizes the short-sightedness of self-crafted vision. I'm referring to the great Hungarian-born chemist-turned-philosopher Michael Polanyi, and the book Len assigned is his magnum opus, *Personal Knowledge*, a book that would challenge the modern assumptions and practices of science. While it is a challenging read, I have come to love this book. But here's the interesting thing: Michael Polanyi did not set out to write a book that would change the underlying approach to science. He certainly didn't set out to make a significant contribution to the study of epistemology . . . he was going to be a chemist.

Before becoming a leader in his field, Michael was born into a secular Jewish home in Hungary in March of 1891. It was the apex of the age of the technical revolution in that region of Western Europe, an area steeped in the legacy of the Enlightenment, and the earlier Renaissance; reason was king. Living as we do in late modernity or postmodernity (a definition still up for debate), where imagination, community, passions, mystery, and doubt are experiencing a revival, it can be challenging for us to imagine just how totalizing "objective" scientific reason was in his day. Science was the new religion. Science and technology were ushering in a new age of humanist hope and unfettered prosperity; or at least, that was the pervasive cultural myth of the time, into which Michael was born. His father bought into this myth. Michael's dad was a high-tech entrepreneur in his day, building much of the Hungarian rail system; his mother established a salon—a place for the exchange of knowledge—that was well known among the intellectuals of Budapest. The world of ideas and technology formed Michael's early years.

What does a kid do when raised in such a context? Well, after leaving teacher's college, Michael went to medical school, to train as a physician. While enrolled, he was an active participant in the Galileo Society, which was a kind of think-tank committed to forming science-driven solutions to the world's greatest unanswered questions. For Michael, the relationship between medical school and the Galileo Society fueled his growing passion for chemistry. Gripped more by physical chemistry than the practice of medicine, he obtained a scholarship to study chemistry at the *Technische Hochschule* in Karlsruhe, Germany, rather than developing a medical practice. Then the First World War hit.

Michael was conscripted to serve as a medical officer and sent to the Serbian front. One can only imagine the challenge of adapting to a war hospital on the front lines of battle, having never previously practiced medicine, but there he was. It didn't take long before Michael became ill and was sent away from the front line to recover. While on sick leave—being the industrious person he was—he wrote his chemistry PhD thesis. This work was impressive enough to be recognized and encouraged by Albert Einstein, and in 1919 he was awarded a doctorate degree. Importantly, this same year, he was also baptized into the church as a follower of Jesus. Michael's story began, set within a world of science and technology, and he was quickly setting himself apart as being among the best and brightest within that reigning paradigm.

Michael was at the top of his game. His research and discoveries were celebrated by the greatest minds in the world, he had a post at a prestigious institution, and some even believed he was well on his way to receiving the Nobel Prize for his work in chemistry (two of his students would eventually receive that award). Yet all this changed with the rise of the Nazi party and the Second World War. Though the seeds may be seen earlier in his life, this Second World War germinated a question that would haunt him for the rest of his life. *How could some of the best minds in the world destroy Europe and perpetuate death and destruction?* At a very basic level he was asking, "What's going on here"? This question burned within him.

If you were at the top of your game, respected by your peers, and sought out by others, what would have to happen for you to give it all up and go in another direction . . . What would have to break? For Michael, what seemed to break was his heart. Though his entire life had been devoted to the study of science, after the apparent complicity of science in the tragedy of WWII, Michael faced a new question: What would he do with his experience of brokenness of the scientific pursuit?[3] He had managed to escape from Germany and had been awarded a post in Manchester,

---

3. Toward the end of Michael's life, at the age of eighty, he published a short essay titled, "Why Did We Destroy Europe?" which bears witness to the prominence of this question after the Second World War. Let me offer a short quote from an earlier, 1957 essay by Polanyi, *Foolishness of History*, highlighting some of his concern. "Yet I know that it was something quite different. Not only when it actually happened; but all along, up to this day—for it still lives in our own blood. It was boundless; it was infinitely potent; it was an act of madness. A great number of men—led by one man possessing genius—set themselves limitless aims that had no bearing at all on reality. They devastated everything in existence and were convinced therefore that the total destruction of existing society and the establishment of their own absolute power on its ruins would bring total happiness to humanity. That was—unbelievable as it may seem—*literally* the whole substance of their projects for a new economic, political, and social system of mankind" (Polanyi, *Foolishness of History*, 33–37).

and, quite frankly, it would have been relatively easy for him to do what everyone expected of him; to simply continue his research. Michael Polanyi did in fact continue his research, but he began a process of living into his brokenness and it changed his life. And in so doing, he made a lasting contribution to the philosophy of science and the field of epistemology (how we know what we know).

Gradually, his interest shifted to political and social sciences and the philosophy of science. In the last third of his academic life, Michael's search for a more truthful knowing within science led to a definitive criterion for knowledge itself. While I will not play out his argument[4] in full (as if I could), it is clear that Michael acted on the question that was burning in his heart: *What is "knowing" if scientific knowledge contributed to such death and destruction in Europe?* He began in earnest to piece together a more truthful account of scientific discovery. Wrestling with the assumed truths of science as it was practiced at the time, he challenged the commonly accepted perspective of his day that the scientist was an objective observer. As Michael leaned into this work, he claimed that the violence of the war sprang not only from nationalism, racism, and hatred but from an impoverished and inhumane epistemology. He argued for a more accurate theory of knowledge. If our knowing is objective—disconnected from our physical bodies and the limitations of ourselves as creatures with real responsibilities to others and to the traditions that form us—then the actions of World War II are inevitable. With such a theory of objectivity there could be no rationale for any limits placed on science and technology.

Why spend so much time offering a glimpse into the story of Michael Polanyi? Because I believe that Michael embodies some of the deepest truths I have learned from Dr. Leonard I. Sweet. Like every person who has ever lived, Michael was born and formed within a specific cultural setting. Later in life he came to trust God's story of redemption. And there came a moment when he experienced brokenness and pain in a way that blew his understanding of the world apart. Yet, Michael did not grieve as one

---

4. In Polanyi's 1946 book *Science, Faith and Society*, Michael challenges the then-dominant models of science as detached and objective. He deepens his argument in his magnum opus, *Personal Knowledge*, in which he lays out an epistemology that presents two kinds of awareness, focal and subsidiary. The types of knowledge grounded in these two kinds of awareness he later called "knowledge by attending to" and "knowledge by relying on." Michael's central thesis is that no knowledge is, or can be, wholly focal. As a follow-up to *Personal Knowledge* he published a little volume called *The Tacit Dimension* in which he further unpacks the tacit knowing as a deep embodied way of knowing.

without hope. He trusted the plot of God's story of redemption enough to be curious about his past and wonder about how his past prepared him for his future. I want to listen thoughtfully to Michael's life as a way of listening to our own. How do we come to trust God's story in the middle of our own experiences of particular places, cultures, and situations that don't unfold according to our personal plans? What path do you follow when your own understanding of the world comes apart? Your spouse dies. Your child develops an addiction to prescription drugs. Crisis erupts, costing you your career. You burn out doing the very thing you understood as your calling. You have a general sense that what you're doing is not working any more, or you are plagued by a new kind of question after an experience of brokenness. Or maybe, in a brief moment of honesty, you discover that your faith is different today than it was before, stirring an internal struggle, with real-world implications for your life and ministry. Basically, your vision for your life is interrupted, and it is raising serious questions about your future. For Michael Polanyi, it was (in part) the horror of WWII that caused him to challenge the fundamental assumptions of the scientific community of his day. For Len Sweet, it was (in part) being personally confronted by the limitations of the modern academy to draw people into following Jesus that invited him to step out of the ivory tower and into the church. What it is for you? Could it be that the death of the vision you had for your life is the birth of a new calling? Here are a few things that I have picked up from my time with Len Sweet that have served me in my experience of life not turning out according to my own personal vision.

Trust the Story

Len bids his readers, hearers, and students to *trust the story*; inviting us to attune our whole being to God's capacious narrative.[5] As you may know, Christians are sometimes mistakenly referred to as a people of the book; we are actually a people of *the story*. Islam is a religion of the book. In Islam the book must be read in its original language, thus limiting access and elevating the culture from which the original language emerges. For Christians, no one human language or culture has a privileged position. Christians are a people of God's story. And God's cosmic narrative of re-creation is experienced in each Christ follower's story of redemption, and in each place where God's will is done on earth as in heaven. The retelling,

5. Sweet, *What Matters Most*.

enactment, and translation of God's narrative invites people to find themselves as characters in God's story; as real contributors to the plot being written by the Author.

You are a story, you are shaped by story, and you live out of and into story. A Christian understanding of trust is trusting God's story over the stories we tell ourselves. A primary function of the gathering of Christians is the re-narration (word), and re-enactment (sacrament) of God's capacious narrative.

The story of God begins in God. Out of God's love God creates and gives life to all. Though human beings attempt to transcend the God-given limitations of our finite being and to avoid the God-given responsibilities as stewards for the flourishing of all creation, God continues to pursue full communion with all of creation. God calls a unique people to Godself to be a blessing to the nations, bearing a living witness to God's redemptive purposes. God even enters the world through God's chosen people in the Lord Jesus Christ; fully God and fully human. And for the first time since the beginning of the story, we see God, and his name is Jesus. We also see what narrative faithfulness looks like: Jesus is present to the will of his Father, and lives in communion with the Spirit, which liberates him to offer himself fully to God's plan, while simultaneously liberating him to be present to others and the systems at play in his cultural context. We see in Jesus what it looks like to trust *the story*. One would think that would be enough, but God in deep wisdom and mercy gives us even more. God gifts us with a glimpse into the fulfillment of *the story*; pulling back the curtain of time for a moment daring us to hope in a future in which all creation will be renewed and restored.

For people of *the story*, our stories are fractals of God's story. Fractals are a mathematical set and are typically self-similar patterns, where self-similar means they are "the same from near as from far"[6]—which is complex language to say that the pattern of the larger whole is repeated and can be seen in each of the smaller parts. More simply, our personal stories of redemption bear witness to God's cosmic story of redemption in all of creation. Therefore, we don't simply hold to God's story with a kind of abstracted hope for eternity. Instead, our lives, lived in the mundane stuff of everyday, bear witness to the truth of God's story playing out now in our own stories. Let's not be glib about this work of God's story in our own. While it is a story of the redemption of brokenness; it is about brokenness

---

6. Gouyet, *Physics and Fractal Structures*.

nonetheless. It is in and through brokenness yielded, like Christ on the cross, that God's redemptive story resonates through our lives. Joseph with his coat of many colors offers one of the most succinct summaries of God's story, "what you meant for evil, God means for good."[7] God is in the business of redemption; even transforming evil intent, false accusations, and torture and death into salvation for all. When we own our brokenness and offer it to the light of Christ, our vocation is revealed; Christian calling is the redemption of brokenness.

If "trust *the story*" is the invitation I've heard from Len, then the next two questions are the tools he's offered me to identify my role in God's unfolding redemptive drama: "Where have you been?" and "Where are you going?" You are always living between these two questions. Wherever you are, and whatever you're doing now, you can look back on your personal story and answer the question, *"Where you have been?"* And whether you're eighteen or eighty-eight, your very breath leaves you pregnant with the second question . . . "Where you are going?"

Where Have You Been?

Stories are always more complex than we tend to believe. No matter how detailed the timeline of your life, the question of where you have been will woo you to reflect even more deeply on your own story. So let me ask, what was happening around you in your formative years? As best as you are able, suspend judgment of the events and listen for the spirit of the era. Understanding your context is a vital part of recognizing how your identity was formed. I encourage you to actually take some time to reflect and write down yours responses to these questions.

What cultural setting were you born into? What was the shape of your built environment and attitudes toward the creational environment? What role did local wisdom play in your education? How were you formed by social movements like civil rights, feminism, military conflicts, LGBTQ rights, and the like? What emotions do you recall around the assassinations of JFK, MLK Jr., John Lennon, or the American Indian Movement of the early 1970s, the LA riots and the beating of Rodney King, the American crackdown on its shared border with Mexico, or even the Challenger space shuttle explosion? If these events don't feel crucial to your formation, what does that tell you? What other events stand out from your own cultural

---

7. Gen 50:19–21, my paraphrase.

context and why? What role might your family's financial class have played in your formation? What was going on around you? What was focused on, what was ignored?

And where was the church in your early experience? How was the spark of your understanding of yourself as a spiritual being stoked within this setting?

Part of being human is the inescapable reality of particularity. You are you. You are not someone else. And you are located in a specific time and place. You are here and not there. While e-communication may cloud this basic reality of embodiment, it is nonetheless true. You are somewhere. Where? What's the story of your place? And while this may be the setting in which your story is launched, there is almost always a twist in the plot.

The setting of your story is the context of God's redemptive plot which is being lived out by one of God's favorite characters—you. Your setting is not simply a series of events to navigate or to try to forget, nor is your setting something to freeze frame for future generations. Rather, it is the very setting in which God is writing God's own story of re-creation. Only you contain the constellation of events, cultural responses to events, and people that make up the formational cocktail that is your life to this moment. What is the redemptive *telos* (the end toward which you are moving) of where you have been? Given that your story is a fractal of God's redemptive narrative, what might the Author be inviting of you?

Where Are You Going?

The flip side of the "Where have you been?" question is the "Where are you going?" question. These two questions dance together inside of Len; after all he is both a historian and a futurist.

He leans back into the question of where we have been as a culturally located church and as individuals, while kicking forward into where we are going as people of the story of God in postmodern culture. The truth is that where we are going is always born out of where we have been. For some, the trajectory is relatively clean and easy to track. For others, the narrative is marked by deliberate moves away from their starting point and numerous diversions along the way.

Back to Michael Polanyi for a moment. After witnessing the death and destruction of WWII, he became convinced that the rootless pursuit of science and technique, without regard for the God-given limitations of human embodiment and particularity, render more plausible the applications of science and technology without respect for the God-given responsibility that human beings have for each other and for God's created world. But this realization of the brokenness of his cultural context didn't cause him to simply quit his work in chemistry. Rather, he leaned back into the assumptions undergirding his discipline and leveraged the discourse models of his scientific community to challenge the precritical assumptions that had enabled the death and destruction of WWII. His thoughtful engagement with where he had come from uniquely prepared him for where he was going.

Where you have been is God's preparation for *where you are going*, if you will dare to trust *the story*, that is, the unfolding of God's story into your own. Is it possible that your place of deepest shame or regret could be pointing toward your future? Could it be that your tomorrow might be connected to your today's experience of brokenness? If "trust *the story*" is the invitation heard from Len, and the questions through which we interpret the story are *"Where have you been?"* and *"Where are you going?"* then the act of trusting has to take place somewhere in that middle space between these two questions. The final question that I have learned from Len is a question for that middle space, it's a semiotic question—a question of meaning making in the wilderness between what has shaped you and what is yet to come. This final question is one that opens us up to see the signs of God presence in the midst of life's unanticipated plot turns.

What's Going On Here?

One of the semiotic questions I gleaned from Len in my study with him is: "What's going on here?" It's a question born of curiosity and humility, and a deep belief that God's story is being written and will be fully realized in spite of apparent evidence—like WWII or personal tragedy—that points to the contrary. It is a question that is resilient to self-pity. It seeks out God's invitation to act and to be different in light of the gospel. As followers of Christ, we ask, "What's going on here?" with faithfulness to the narrative of the life, death, and resurrection of God in the God-man Jesus Christ.

In the middle space between the questions "Where have you been?" and "Where are you going?" we can call out with both lament and expectation to ask God about the brokenness, "What's going on here?" It's a question that, when asked with the Spirit of God, has a way of further weaving the asker into the fractal pattern of God's redemptive narrative. As such, followers of Christ can lean into such a question with deep hope that, though the brokenness of our context and our personal story can at times take us to our breaking point, God's narrative of the renewal of all things is already and always present. This is at least part of why Len's career as a historian and a futurist gave way to his vocation as a Christian semiotician; reading the signs of *the story* in the world. His calling is to understand where we have been, asking the question "What's going on here?" and in light of the hope of Christ, to look to the future of where we are going.

And while we only ever arrive at partial answers to the question of "What's going on here?" we have enough to move forward into the question of "Where are you going?" Faith does not require absolute certainty; instead faith woos us to trust what we can sense of the story of God's redemption, inviting hope in the resurrection of Jesus, freeing us to explore our experience of brokenness. Asking the question "What's going on here?" from that middle space of honestly facing the brokenness of where we have been and living into a gospel response as a way forward does not always win us favor. And it doesn't always take us where we might expect it to. Michael Polanyi lost the admiration of some colleagues in the world of chemistry; he lived on the outer fringe of the philosophical community during his life. Today we know that *Personal Knowledge* occupies an important place in the field of epistemology, but Michael didn't know the impact his work would have. All he knew was that he and the scientific community needed a more robust understanding of knowledge. And that maybe, if he offered up his vision of his future he might have something to contribute. It seems crisis often serves as an invitation to alter one's vocational direction.

In preparation for this chapter I read Len Sweet's first thirty-four books in chronological order. Fascinating! As I did, I detected a significant shift. It may not be quite as dramatic as Michael's shift from chemistry to philosophy, but it is a change in direction nonetheless. I noticed the shift in his focus with the publication of his 1995 *Strong in Broken Places*. I'd describe the shift as moving away from furthering an academic conversation to very intentionally reshaping the conversation for all who are seeking to follow Jesus in a rapidly changing cultural context. Initially I became curious about what might have been happening in or around his Len's life, but as I continued to read his subsequent books my curiosity morphed into gratitude. On making this observation I sensed a parallel between Len and Michael that I hadn't noticed before: at the top of their fields, something happens inviting them to listen afresh to God's call on their lives, and they courageously respond to the invitation of God to follow a different path, and in so doing gift the world with a body of work that likely would not have existed if they had stuck to their original vision. I have little knowledge of what it cost Len to make this shift, but I do know that the academy is not always kind to those who break ranks and begin to write for the broader community of the people of God.

And this brings us to back to your story. Before anticipating where you are going, I encourage you to take some time in that middle space to explore and write about the pattern of *the story* and wonder how it might be unfolding in your story.

How do you stay in this middle space to hold the question "What's going on here?" What might it look like for you to trust *the story*? Can you imagine your personal story or the story of your place being a fractal of God's capacious narrative of redemption? If so, given the reality of where you've been, where are you going?

Here's the deal, whatever you signed up for when you followed Christ with your life, it is not likely that your life is what you expected it would be. So the question is, "What's going on here?" What is going on in your context? What's going on in your own life? What is God inviting of you with the time you have remaining? In light of where you have been and the radical changes that have come your way, what must you be about if you are to be faithfully present to the story God is writing in your life? I suppose you could stick to the vision of your life you had wished for, but what if you didn't? What if you listened to your experience of brokenness inviting the Holy Spirit to reveal the contours of your future through it? What will you do with the plot changes of your story? What will you do with the brokenness you've experienced? *The story* as we have seen through Michael Polanyi's story, invites us to move deeper into the darkness of our experience of brokenness and, in so doing, we witness God doing a new thing. Resurrection hope invites followers of Jesus to lean in and engage our context and story rather than run from brokenness.

Trust *the story*; God is making all things new. With the freedom of the power of God's story, interrogate yourself: where have you been, how have you been formed, and how might your unique formation in light of *the story* embolden you to live into where you are going? All the while, hear the question, "What's going on here?" How might you discern with the people of God, wise and courageous ways of being in the world that bear witness—like a fractal—to God's capacious story of redemption?

One of the primary lessons I've learned from my mentor Len Sweet is that brokenness is nothing to hide; rather, in God's economy my brokenness is the very thing God redeems. In fact, it is through brokenness redeemed in Christ that my life reflects the very story God is authoring in all of creation. Trust *the story*!

Bibliography

Gouyet, Jean-François. *Physics and Fractal Structures*. New York: Masson Springer, 1996.

Polanyi, Michael. "The Foolishness of History." *Encounter* 9 (1957) 33–37.

———. *Personal Knowledge: Towards a Post-Critical Philosophy*. Chicago: University of Chicago Press, 1958.

———. *Science, Faith, and Society*. London: Bles, 1946.

Sweet, Leonard I. *Strong in Broken Places: A Theological Reverie on the Ministry of George Everett Ross*. Akron, OH: University of Akron Press, 1995.

———. *What Matters Most: How We Got the Point but Missed the Person*. Colorado Springs: WaterBrook, 2004.

6

The EPIC World of Anglican Worship

Todd Hunter, DMin

WITHIN ANCIENT ISRAEL THE men of Issachar were described as leaders "who understood the signs of the times and knew the best course for Israel to take [NLT]; [who] knew what Israel should do [NIV]; [who were] men who understood both the times and Israel's duties" (1 Chron 12:32 *The Message*). Len Sweet stands in a long line of godly learners who loved the times in which God created them to live, who resisted the urge to easy cynicism about the church, and yet refused to be suspicious of societal change and slide into antagonism with their secular culture. Sweet manages to be a man of *our period* while challenging readers and students through the best thinkers of the *past*.

Ancient and Present Reformers

Sweet's work mirrors that of Thomas Cranmer, the key leader in the English reformation, Archbishop of Canterbury and the senior author of a way of life and public worship entitled *The Book of Common Prayer*. Hundreds of years ago Cranmer was a man of *his* times. He grasped both the content and the implications of the continental Reformation for his people, for his time. But Cranmer didn't solely focus on the zeitgeist of his age and the in-your-face tension between the Continental Reformers and the Roman Church.

Cranmer made two key moves of which I imagine Dr. Sweet would loudly applaud. I'm thinking here of Sweet's leadership analogy of swinging.

That in doing life and ministry there is *a simultaneous kicking-back/leaning-forward and kicking-forward/leaning-back*. Cranmer reached back in order to swing forward into a preferred future.[1] The *reach back* was a move to the early church fathers as a way to adjudicate the theological debates and distresses of his contemporaries and the confusions warring about in his own mind. Simultaneously, Cranmer, unlike some of his hesitant colleagues, swung forward out of the classical Old French and Latin languages that had dominated the religious past. In so doing, he swung into an uncertain future marked by the brewing new street language of his time and his people—English.

Using the present day insights of missiology, we could say that Cranmer understood the concept of *heart language*; that people come to Christ best, most intuitively, when they have Christ presented to them in words, idioms, images and symbols that have instinctive, intuitive resonance with a given culture. Cranmer was willing to bet his reputation and that of his church on *the people's language* being spoken in the street, not the language that dominated history and high-society places of higher learning. It is both ironic and instructive that we now venerate what Cranmer wrote in his 1549 *Book of Common Prayer* (and the versions that followed) so much that the Anglican Church is often afraid to change *it*.

An EPIC Conversation

EPIC: just two vowels and two consonants. But those four letters, strung together in that order, have been instructive for many churches struggling to interface with our present age: the wired, app-driven, social media new world. They are in my view four of the most impactful letters Len Sweet ever wrote.[2] Those four letters, E-P-I-C, are meant to teach the church how to carry out the mission of Jesus in the *way* of Jesus. Jesus taught his followers to be *in* the world—using its street languages, but *not* of it—in terms of its guiding values and teleology (John 17:14–15).

Sweet, a futurist and an evangelist at heart, consistently asks two questions: What are the marks of our world? How are we to be in it, but not of it? This two-pronged process of discovery yielded his EPIC breakthrough.

Sweet's EPIC theory calls for missional Christian worship and life that is *experiential*—facilitating an experience of God, not just delivering

1. Leonard Sweet, in discussion with the author.
2. See Sweet, *Post-modern Pilgrims*.

information about him; *participatory*—not merely performance or stage-driven worship in which something is done to you; *image-driven*—not merely word-based religious teaching; and *connected*—not simply individual-focused spirituality but worship that is communal and that is simultaneously translated for and connected to the culture. The acronym EPIC launched a missional, ecclesiastical and worship discussion that is now well more than a decade long. The conversation is rooted in insights about the marks of the early twenty-first century:

> *Experiential:* Child-focused eateries like Chuck E. Cheese and coffee shops like Starbucks are no longer selling pizza and coffee, they are providing experiences. Major league sports stadiums and arenas and whole shopping malls are increasingly in the experience business.
>
> *Participatory:* A few years ago no one had ever heard of reality television shows in which viewers determine future programing by voting on who stays on the show or who goes home. Presently, participatory programming dominates viewership. *Wikipedia* is a participatory encyclopedia. Craigslist is a participatory form of the old advertising section found in newspapers. Angie's List is like a citywide backyard fence over which neighbors can share information about which tradesmen and vendors are most reliable and who offers the most reasonable pricing.
>
> *Image-rich:* Today even gas stations provide small screens on the pump that pulsate images out to drivers standing idle next to their cars. Increasingly anyone trying to communicate or sell anything knows that *seeing* is a core pathway to understanding.
>
> *Connective:* Group dating is now the norm; front porches and patios in the form of outdoor rooms are in big demand. People crave the connectional vibe seen in old movies set in the South: full of warm human touch and generous conversation.

It would be fair for a reader at this point to ask: what do those social observations have to do with gospel ministry? Jesus called his first friends to follow him and to become *fishers of men*. There is one thing every fisherman knows: you catch fish on their terms, not yours. This is not an argument for compromising the gospel. It is a simple statement of fact. If the larger fish are eating tiny fish feeding in the deep, cold water where the current is less fierce, a fisherman needs to find a way to present the correct bait in a form in which the fish will bite. If the fish are only eating early in the morning as the sun comes up, the fisherman can't roll out of bed at ten in the morning and expect to catch anything. Any approach other than "on their terms" will run afoul of Jesus' caution about not casting pearls before swine. Swine cannot be nourished by pearls, but only on bits of food made especially for them. EPIC fish will only eat EPIC bait. We need to learn to fish with such bait.

Thomas Cranmer Was EPIC

Employing a bold and tongue-in-cheek anachronism, we could say that Thomas Cranmer had, in the sense of being *willing to change* for the sake of loving his culture, EPIC instincts. Writing in the preface to his first version (1549) of *The Book of Common Prayer*, Cranmer said:

> It is a most invaluable part of that blessed "liberty wherewith Christ hath made us free," that in his worship different forms and usages may without offense be allowed, provided the substance of the Faith be kept entire . . . [that] by common consent and authority [this prayer book], may be altered, abridged, enlarged, amended, or otherwise disposed of, as may seem most convenient *for the edification of the people, according to the various exigency of times and occasions.* (emphasis added)

Cramer was concerned that his flock didn't understand Latin, that at best they "heard with theyr eares onely; and their hartes, spirite, and minde, have not been edified thereby."[3] I perceive in Sweet's work a heart like Cranmer's—namely, that postmodern people no longer understand or relate to the information-based, stage-driven, word-rich and individualist approach to the gospel.

If we give it a moment of thought, the Cranmer-Sweet connection should not surprise us. Gospel leaders of the church have always cared about how to best communicate with the culture in which they found themselves. This is true from Jesus, to the apostles, to Paul, to the church fathers, to the reformers, to the American frontier revivalists, to Billy Graham and finally to the sophisticated, Spirit-inspired youth leaders of today. No form of evangelism ever arose from a vacuum. Every form of communicating

---

3. *Booke of the common prayer* (1549).

the gospel has risen from a precise and specific social and cultural context. Understanding this, and being willing to take the risks associated with innovation is part of the genius of leaders like Cranmer and Sweet.

It is a safe historical bet to confidently say that Thomas Cranmer was not trying to be relevant, culturally current, provide alternative worship, be church-next or be emergent—at least not in the popular book- and conference-driven way we might think about it. Cranmer was a deeply spiritual leader and a seriously intellectual follower of Jesus who, knowing he was alive at a key moment in history, was trying to disciple his nation to Jesus. To put it crudely, Cranmer was trying to spread a virus—the virus of the orthodox, heart-religion of following Jesus.

Why Be EPIC?

To my mind Cranmer was the Billy Graham, Dallas Willard and Eugene Peterson of his day—all wrapped into one remarkable person. I mean to say by this that Cranmer was simultaneously an evangelist, a philosopher-apologist and thoughtful pastor. Such a man is not found too often in the history of the church. Making use of Cranmer and his *Book of Common Prayer*, I now turn toward discovering how the EPIC theory put forward by Sweet explains what Cranmer was up to in his day and simultaneously provides a model for ministry today.

How did multisensory worship become a form of emergent or alternative worship? It is actually ancient, going back past the beginning of the church to the festivals and rituals of Israel. Yet it seemed like out-of-the-box thinking when Sweet first argued for EPIC worship and an EPIC form of church life. The ideas conveyed in EPIC could be more properly attributed to the ancient church than they are to the angst of emergent youth leaders.

Loving and worshipping God, as the Shema insists, involves a person's heart, soul, and strength. Jesus, during a typical argument with his contemporaries, was asked, "What is the greatest commandment?" Jesus answered using the Shema and added the component of the mind: "Love the Lord your God with all your heart and with all your soul and with all your mind and with all your strength. The second is this: 'Love your neighbor as yourself.' There is no commandment greater than these" (Mark 12:30–31 NIV).

The Shema and the Great Commandment alert us to the truth that we are to love God as integrated and whole human beings. Such a life is, in my view best facilitated by EPIC worship. Worship as telling the story of what God intended, what he has done over time, where the story is moving to in the future and how humans can get in on that story through Jesus Christ. EPIC worship keeps us connected to the story and unfolding drama of Scripture. It keeps us announcing, embodying and demonstrating what God is up to on the earth—right now and into the future.

Now let's turn to Anglican history and theology to discover a huge treasure chest for doing evangelism and discipleship found in the EPIC worship of the *Book of Common Prayer*.

EPIC Worship

Let's unpack the ways in which Cranmer was EPIC.

> *Eucharist (Holy Communion):* Take and eat . . . take and drink. What could be more experiential, participative and connective/communal than the weekly (or daily) sharing in the Table of Jesus? As an Anglican bishop and minister, every week I actually take bread and break it. I lift a heavy cup made of precious metal. After praying over the elements I break bits of the bread and place them lovingly and worshipfully upon the flesh of the humbly upturned palms of those who have come to dine at the Table of Jesus. On the road to Emmaus, finding ideas about Jesus confusing at best and bankrupt at worst, the brokenhearted and wandering disciples recognize Jesus in the breaking of bread. That was an EPIC conversion, and EPIC renewal of faith.
>
> Why does Eucharist have such power? That question leads to beautiful and deep matters, matters beyond the scope of this chapter. But one thing needs to be said: some actions are themselves an EPIC form of communication that is more powerful than mere words. A handshake is more than two hands in motion—it is my pledge to do as I say or a way to offer my warm greeting. A kiss is more than two lips touching—it is an EPIC rendering of marital, familial or friendly love. Cutting a ribbon goes way beyond sharp metal pressed against thinly stretched material to an EPIC way of inaugurating a new reality now open to us. Eucharist is EPIC not least because it gives participants an ongoing and growing experience of participation in the life, formation and mission of Christ.
>
> *Ancient Anglican Rhythms:* Our world needs to hear and embody a new story. The present story, dominated by its current

characters and plot lines is not very attractive. More and more people wonder: is there more available to humans than politics, economics, education, medicine and religion as we now know them? The answer announced in Jesus' gospel of the in-breaking of the kingdom of God is—yes! But people need access to a transcendent story. Where do they find it? Thomas Cranmer, in the *Book of Common Prayer*, provided a few EPIC on-ramps to the Grand Narrative. First *a church calendar* that annually inculcates in us the truth that the unfolding story of God begins with the Advent of Jesus (his first and second coming), the manifestation of Jesus as the Christ, to Lent and then Easter and finally to the ordinary time of growth in Christ. Throughout this calendar we hear God's story told in lectionary readings and personally commit to live in this story through the daily prayers. Going beyond acquiring mere knowledge, this annual rhythm is an EPIC source of authority and wisdom.

Creed: Postmodern pilgrims wonder if anything is really true, anything in which one can place solid confidence. The Creed ("The Apostles'" or "Nicene"), said daily or weekly in unison with a group of Jesus-followers, is an EPIC source of truth amidst postmodern epistemological angst. As the main teaching minister in an Anglican church, caring deeply for the spiritual growth of those with whom I worship, I sometimes find myself saying to spiritual seekers: Just say the creed with us. You don't have to get it all at once. You can doubt. You may experience some confusion or cognitive dissonance. But go on the ride suggested by the creed. Unclench your jaw. The bulging of your facial muscles screams aloud your hatred of religious parents or an abusive church experience. Get your hands off the neck of the church you've wanted to strangle. If, over time, you come to find that there is something between you and God, well . . . become a radical with us: find and follow Jesus in the safety of this seeking community and in the story of Jesus outlined by the creeds. "If you do", I tell them, "you will become more human, more alive than you could have ever dreamed!"

The Lectionary/Ministry of the Word: Every week in Anglican worship we have four readings from the Bible: a Psalm, an Old

Testament and New Testament reading and reading from the Gospels. These readings are done *EPICally*. As a gathered people we recite the appointed Psalm through various responsive forms as a sign of unspeakable respect for Jesus—his words and works—we surround the Gospel reading with sung worship and stand for its reading. We comment on the passages in a sermon and then provide a time of silence that we might hear and ponder the voice of the Spirit as he applies the readings and sermon to our lives. This all adds up to an EPIC way to reshape a worldview and to invite worshippers, as followers of Jesus, into the story the readings tell.

The Prayer of Confession and Absolution: Postmodern pilgrims find truth to be elusive, especially when it comes to finding, grasping and committing to a moral vision. The education from cable news over the last couple decades makes things truly appear to be relative, contextual and perspectival. How can one know what is wrong or right? Where do we look for answers? If I find answers, does that mean that I'll become an arrogant religious extremist or a hardheaded bigot? As a pastoral spiritual director, I find the Prayer of Confession to be an EPIC way of getting at this very real challenge. The words, prayed in common are simple, evocative and image-rich:

> Most merciful God, we confess that we have sinned against you in thought, word, and deed, by what we have done, and by what we have left undone. We have not loved you with our whole heart; we have not loved our neighbors as ourselves. We are truly sorry and we humbly repent. For the sake of your Son Jesus Christ, have mercy on us and forgive us; that we may delight in your will, and walk in your ways, to the glory of your Name. Amen.[4]

I am sometimes asked if, on the contrary to being beautiful, if all of this can, over time, become rote? I often respond with, "Of course! Any kind of worship or prayer can become a hollow ritual."

Debriefing once with a college-aged person at church, she said to me, "Why would I want to pray using those words—they are not mine.

---

4. *Book of Common Prayer* (1979).

Someone else wrote them a long time ago. It would not be *authentic* for me to pray them."

"Ok", I said to her, "I get it. Could you please pray for me now in words that are your own—not words you learned from someone else as the proper way to address God?" I wasn't trying to be cute or to trap her. It was an honest response to a genuine question. She quickly realized that "Father, Wejuss ask you to . . . " did not in any way surpass or improve on the prepared prayer that has been prayed by the church all over the world for generations.

In that moment I had an epiphany. I wrote out on a piece of paper a few of the words from the prayer: "what/we/have/done/left undone . . . " Spinning the paper around so my friend could see it, I drew buckets under each of the words and said, "What if each of these words is so full of meaning that you could reach in and find what you want to say, what is real to you, and then use the written confession as a launching pad for words that come from your own heart and soul?"

At that moment we both began to see the substantial spiritual potential in active participation with what has been written in the past and prayed for through the centuries. On some days the prescribed word *done* brings before my mind a whole collage of sin. Other times the prearranged term *undone* yields a heartbreak of missed divine appointments that might may made me into an agent of Divine healing, wisdom or deliverance from injustice or darkness. We both sat back in our chairs realizing that we just shared a moment of transformative insight.

Something similar happened the night I had a class from a local university sit in on our Ash Wednesday service at Holy Trinity Church. Our worship tends to be quiet and contemplative at all times, and especially during the penitential seasons of the church year—like Lent. Not much in church life is more EPIC than, after sitting quietly with God about what is real about you, rising from your seat, walking down the aisle in front of everyone, kneeling before the minister and having ashes marked on your forehead—ashes that were created by burning the palms from the prior year's Palm Sunday service. As the ashes are applied one of these sentences are said over the worshippers: *Remember that thou art dust, and to dust thou shalt return*, or *Repent and believe the Gospel*.

The following Wednesday night, during a debriefing with the class, a student said, "You are asking us to slow down too fast! My mind wanders when I have to stop my frantic pace, walk in the door and settle down for the quiet prelude." Most of the students enrolled in the course attend a local mega-church. Their worship services are comprised of a loud rock band leading thirty to forty minutes of worship music followed by a Bible study given in the contemporary, casual and humorous rhetorical style that is widespread in Southern California.

I then asked the student if he ever found his mind wondering during the worship sets at his church. I could see by the look in his eyes that he was having an epiphany of his own. Finally, he stammered out his enlightenment: "Yes; my mind does wonder a lot during the singing!"

"Perhaps," I responded, "the problem is not in the silence or in the loud rock music, but in our noisy minds? What can we do about our minds? How can we be at peace, at rest and centered in Jesus?"

Sacramental Liturgy: EPIC but Not Perfect

Over the last four years, learning my way into the sacramental and liturgical world, I have had many moments like the two I just recounted. Sacramental worship, which uses the material world to communicate spiritual realities of and from God, really is EPIC in the way Sweet would want us the think. A liturgical and sacramental worship service is truly *experiential*. Nothing in what we do suggests that a worshipper should "sit back and enjoy the service."

In sharp contrast, everything in a liturgical service says, "sit up, pay attention and *participate*." The whole service is *image-rich*: the table, the vestments of the ministers, the processional cross, the alter lights, the Gospel held high as we stand to hear it, the bread, the cup, etc. Finally, everything is done in a *connective*, communal way. Liturgy is what the *whole* people do. We pray in unison. We read the Psalm antiphonally.

Having now been sufficiently optimistic about the EPIC value and potential inherent in liturgical worship, two words of caution or *reality* are in order. First, the liturgy is not some form of ancient magic that automatically produces spiritual fruit. To be spiritually fruitful it needs two things: (1) leadership by Spirit-inspired, Spirit-led clergy and lay people and (2) genuine, honest participation by worshippers. Additionally, liturgical worship ceases to be EPIC and falls into the crosshairs of its worst critiques when it becomes fussy, nitpicking or overelaborate. When it slips to those places, it loses its unforced rhythms of elegance. When worship becomes frilly, showy and ornate it sucks all the air out of the room—air for humans to breath and for the presence of the Spirit to blow his converting, renewing and healing breath upon us.

EPIC Worship Leads to an EPIC Life

Religion can never be non-EPIC, reduced to giving mental assent to certain points of important doctrine. For instance, at the end of the Sermon on the Mount, Jesus shows without a doubt that he is interested in something experiential, something participatory, and something connective/communal when he says:

> These words I speak to you are not incidental additions to your life, homeowner improvements to your standard of living. They are foundational words, words to build a life on. If you work these words into your life, you are like a smart carpenter who built his house on solid rock. Rain poured down, the river flooded, a tornado hit—but nothing moved that house. It was fixed to the rock. But if you just use my words in Bible studies and don't work them into your life, you are like a stupid carpenter who built his house on the sandy beach. When a storm rolled in and the waves came up, it collapsed like a house of cards. (Matt 7:24–27 *The Message*)

It is clear, in Sweet's terms, that Jesus is looking for an EPIC response to his teaching. Jesus is striving to create a community of people who experience and participate in his teaching through actions based on trust, reliance and confidence in him as their teacher for what it means to live life in the kingdom of God.

Paul shoots for the same EPIC response. When he is done with his famous writings in Romans chapters 1 through 11, he turns to the "so what?" of his doctrine in chapter 12: "So here's what I want you to do, God helping you: Take your everyday, ordinary life—your sleeping, eating, going-to-work, and walking-around life—and place it before God as an offering" (Rom 12:1–2).

For Paul, EPIC worship is the daily and weekly rhythm by which we come to appreciate God, loving and valuing him above all else and finding meaning for our lives within his purposes for humanity. Such worship overflows naturally to our everyday ordinary experience, our participation in our present world until we become Jesus' cooperative friends, ambassadors of his kingdom, joining him in the renewal of all creation. The end of our story suggests life stoked by EPIC worship of God becomes a never-ending partnership with him. In one of his last visions John of Patmos saw that the people of heaven will rule and reign with God forever and ever in the new heaven and the new earth (Rev 22:5).

That is the grand, epic and eternal adventure to which EPIC worship leads.

Bibliography

The Book of Common Prayer and Administration of the Sacraments and other Rites and Ceremonies of the Church. New York: Church Publishing, 1979.

The booke of the common prayer and administracion of the sacramentes, and other rites and ceremonies of the churche after the use of the Churche of England. 1549. http://justus.anglican.org/resources/bcp/1549/front_matter_1549.htm.

Sweet, Leonard I. *Post-modern Pilgrims.* Nashville: Broadman & Holman, 2000.

7

Every Bush is Burning

Thomas E. Ingram, DMin

ONE DAY IN 1988, some ministry coworkers of mine attended a conference hosted by First Methodist Church in Tulsa, Oklahoma. Upon their return, one of them walked into my office, plopped down a cassette tape[1] and said: "You need to listen to this, you will love this guy." The tape was an audio recording of Len Sweet . . . and thus my journey began.

I cannot remember what was on that tape, but whatever it was put me on notice; Len Sweet was someone I needed to pay attention to. And that is just what I have done in the years since that fateful day.

One of the things I find compelling about Len is not only what he says but also how he says it. His use of language is artful and imaginative and filled with the mysteries of God. When you read his books, it is hard not to get caught up in the near breathless enthusiasm of his delivery, as if there were not enough words or time to say everything that needs to be said. Len's insights come at you from every direction leaving you no other recourse than to stand with him in awe of a God that is more than any of us can imagine. You see, in Len's world everything seems to resonate with the holy vibrations of a creative God inviting us into a grand adventure. An expression of this resonance can be found in Len's book *Nudge*, where he suggests: "Every bush is burning"[2] . . . all of creation announcing, pronouncing and inviting us into the glorious presence of our creator. I like the idea of a world filled with burning bushes, because . . . on the best of days . . . this is my world as well.

1. Ancient technology only a few of us will remember . . .
2. Sweet, *Nudge*, 27.

Understanding in a World of Burning Bushes

This reference to a burning bush of course refers to Moses' experience while tending his father-in-law's sheep at Horeb.[3] As you will remember, Moses, while minding his business, came upon a bush that was blazing with fire and yet not consumed.[4] When he approached this curious sight, God spoke directly to him, informing Moses he had been chosen to free God's people from the oppressive rule of Pharaoh.[5] Moses reluctantly agreed and the rest, as we know, is history.

The New Testament tells another "burning bush" story of sorts in the events surrounding the Holy Spirit's manifestation at Pentecost. This event, however, differs from Moses' in that it was not the private experience of a lone individual, but rather a public manifestation in the midst of a community of believers. As the story goes, the disciples were "gathered together in one place"[6] when what appeared to be tongues of fire rested upon each of them and they began speaking in foreign tongues.[7] The initial reaction to this was somewhat less than enthusiastic with some believing the explanation could be found in the disciples being drunk quite early in the day.[8] Confusion apparently reigned until Peter was able to address the crowd, suggesting the correct explanation did not reside in drunken disciples, but instead could be more accurately understood as God's spirit poured out upon all flesh:[9] the manifestation of that which Jesus had promised.[10] This suggestion must have been understood and accepted by the community, for there were several thousand of them baptized later in the day.[11]

We see another example of community discernment as a way to understand a theological event or issue in the way Paul resolved a challenge concerning circumcision of new believers. Apparently, while Paul and Barnabas were visiting the church in Antioch, a group arrived from Judea insisting, "Unless you are circumcised, according to the custom taught by

---

3. Exod 3:1.
4. Exod 3:2.
5. Exod 3.
6. Acts 2:1.
7. Acts 2:4.
8. Acts 2:13.
9. Acts 2:17–19.
10. Acts 1:4–5.
11. Acts 2:41.

Moses, you cannot be saved."[12] After what the text calls "sharp dispute and debate,"[13] the decision was made to send Paul and Barnabas back to Jerusalem so they could present the issue to the apostles and other elders of the church.[14] Once they arrived in Jerusalem, the matter was discussed and the decision was made to send Paul, Barnabas, and others back to the church at Antioch with a letter containing the following statement on the issue: "It seemed good to the Holy Spirit and to us not to burden you with anything beyond the following requirements: You are to abstain from food sacrificed to idols, from blood, from the meat of strangled animals and from sexual immorality. You will do well to avoid these things. Farewell."[15] And with that decree, there was no doubt, much rejoicing.

One element both of these New Testament stories hold in common is the way in which understanding, discernment, and response was determined in the midst of community. Acknowledgment of this brings forth a question: How do we understand, discern, and respond to the promptings of the Holy Spirit today?

In personal matters, our confirmation seems to arrive via an ever-increasing familiarity with the experience of the Holy Spirit as we have heard this voice before and have tested the waters upon which it has called us to walk.

But, in a larger context, our ability to discern the voice of the Holy Spirit from amongst the "inspired" cacophony of voices within the church suggesting we do this, or do that, or move in this direction, or stop doing that, or change nothing at all, seems to be disadvantaged due to our limited opportunities for community discernment . . . those forums in which we are able to eventually conclude: "It seemed good to the Holy Spirit and to us."[16]

Opportunity for community discernment is made difficult by the way in which we gather together as a church in events that are typically more scripted than inspired leaving little space from which the Holy Spirit can make its presence known to the community at large. We are further challenged in this endeavor by the distance we tend to place between others and ourselves, as most of us no longer live in a community of believers, but

---

12. Acts 15:1 NIV.
13. Acts 15:2.
14. Acts 15:2.
15. Acts 15:28–29.
16. Acts 15:28.

increasingly live disconnected lives that embrace the more individualistic aspects of Western culture.

This is not to suggest the Holy Spirit is incapable of overcoming distance, time, or our short attention spans. However it does suggest, in a noisy world that increasingly distances us from one another, our ability to interpret and confirm that which the Holy Spirit is calling us toward is increasingly challenged.

Proxemics

We can better understand distance and its impact on community through Dr. Ed Hall's concept of proxemics; a term that refers to the "theories of man's use of space as a specialized elaboration of culture."[17] Based upon his research, Dr. Hall has proposed the existence of four distinct social spaces in which humans interact with one another: *intimate, personal, social, and public*.[18]

Intimate Space

Intimate space ranges from physical contact to a distance of eighteen inches[19] and is a zone typically reserved for those who are intimately acquainted with one another. In the zone of intimate space, "olfaction, heat from the other person's body, sound, smell, and feel of the breath all combine to signal unmistakable involvement with another body."[20]

Personal Space

Personal space occupies the region from a *close* personal space of 1.5 to 2.5 feet to a *distant* personal space of 2.5 to four feet.[21] This is a distance we can call *within arms reach*. The co-locating of two individuals within arms

---

17. Hall, *Hidden Dimension*, 1.
18. Ibid., 114.
19. Ibid., 117.
20. Ibid., 116.
21. Ibid., 120.

reach of one another would signal the nature of their relationship in both the professional and personal sphere.[22]

Social Space

Next we encounter *social space*, which is defined by a close social distance of four to seven feet to a greater social distance of seven to twelve feet.[23] In the office, the arrangement of the desks and furniture in the conference room tend to conform to *social* distances, as does the typical seating in our living rooms. Interestingly, the proximal distances found in our kitchens conform more toward *personal* distances, which may help to explain why the kitchen is always the most crowded room in the house when friends visit . . . that, and the *proximity* to food of course.

Public Space

Public space is defined as a close distance of twelve to twenty-five feet to a further distance of twenty-five feet or more.[24] At these distances communication is difficult, if not impossible, without the use of some sort of technical aid. We see evidence of this in attempts to bridge the distance between the stage and viewer in large churches or arenas when video screens are utilized as a way to return the viewer to a *proximal* distance more appropriate to the relationship they are attempting to create.

Using a video screen to bridge spatial zones in an effort to achieve greater intimacy is an example of what Dr. Hall calls *extensions*.[25] Extensions are ways in which we attempt to "improve or specialize various functions."[26] For example, a shovel would be an extension as it extends our ability to dig; a hammer and saw would be extensions as they extend our ability to build; and a computer would likewise be an extension as it can extend the capabilities of our brain.[27]

---

22. Ibid.
23. Ibid., 121.
24. Ibid., 123–24.
25. Ibid., 3.
26. Ibid.
27. Ibid.

Based upon Dr. Hall's concept of extensions, we can view the Internet as a kind of extension . . . a tool that enables an ever-growing population of individuals to connect and collaborate in a *proximal* space appropriate for those types of interactions. It is a space separate and distinct from Dr. Hall's four zones. It is a space we can call *digital space*.

Digital space is paradoxical. *Digital space* is close and yet far. *Digital space* is private and yet public. It is a space in which the experience of proximity gets blurred. As such, *digital space* is a new kind of proximal zone enabled by a technological age.

So the question arises, is there a way to reconnect a Westernized body of Christ in *digital space* that better enables us to understand, discern, and respond to the voice of the Holy Spirit calling out to the church today?

Crowdsourcing may offer just such a solution.

Little Did He Know

Several years ago I was meeting with the executive pastor of a church to discuss what I thought was the possibility of my joining them in some pastoral capacity. In contrast, he was under the impression we were meeting to discuss my working with them to direct the television and media efforts of their ministry. It did not take long for us to figure out we were not talking about the same thing and so our conversation gracefully moved to discussing what was stirring in our hearts concerning how to "do church" more effectively.

Based upon our conversation, he suggested I read a book called *Crowdsourcing*, by Jeff Howe. At the time, I had no idea what crowdsourcing was but was anxious to find out and so I ordered the book when I got home. While I did not recognized it at the time, that casual suggestion of reading material turned out to be a *burning bush* that would influence the direction of my life for years to come. Now let's flash forward a couple of years to where I began my doctor of ministry studies in semiotics and future studies under the mentorship of Dr. Leonard Sweet at George Fox Evangelical Seminary.

At the initial dinner gathering of our cohort, Len posed a question to the group: "How would you like to help me write a book?" Len's vision for coauthorship included not only the members of our cohort but also expanded to include anyone who wished to participate. Since Len had asked me to serve as his teaching assistant for the cohort, I began to investigate the ways in which we could make this work. I remembered crowdsourcing, which appeared to be the perfect solution. And so, with the help of Dr. Loren Kerns, the director of the doctor of ministry program at GFES, we were able to secure an academic license with a company that provides crowdsourcing platforms called IdeaScale.[28] A few weeks later we launched our project called *The 100 Words That Make Us Christian*, which resultantly served as the inspiration for my dissertation.

Introduction to Crowdsourcing

Crowdsourcing is a term we see bantered about more and more often these days . . . oftentimes wrongly associated with any endeavor that involves a crowd working toward some sort of goal. As a way for us to unite around a common understanding, let's take a look at the underlying science behind crowdsourcing as well as how it is currently being used in the marketplace.

Collaborative Network Organization

Crowdsourcing is a way in which people can work together in what is called a collaborative network organization. According to Professor William Dutton, there are three types of collaborative network organizations, or CNOs.[29]

> 1.0 CNO—primarily concerned with the broadcasting or sharing of information.[30]

> 2.0 CNO—utilizes social networks to enable group formation and communication.[31]

> 3.0 CNO—establishes networks that enable individuals to work together through cooperative actions.[32]

It is the 3.0 type of CNOs that enable what Dr. Scott Page, a professor of complex systems, political science, and economics at the University of

---

28. See http://ideascale.com.
29. Dutton, *Wisdom of Collaborative Network Organizations*, 216.
30. Ibid.
31. Ibid.
32. Ibid.

Michigan, calls *distributed co-creation*[33] or as we more commonly know it: crowdsourcing.

Wikipedia is a good example of a *distributed co-creation* (crowdsourcing) project in that it enables members of a 3.0 network organization to collaborate in the creation of a resource with great diversity and depth. Now, it would be natural to assume the social anarchy of the Internet might negate any confidence one might place in the accuracy of the articles on *Wikipedia*, however, research conducted by *Nature* magazine shows the accuracy of *Wikipedia* is comparable to that of the *Encyclopedia Britannica*[34] with "2.92 mistakes per article for Britannica and 3.86 for Wikipedia."[35] In their research, *Nature* also surveyed over one thousand of its contributing authors and discovered approximately 70 percent consult *Wikipedia* with more than 80 percent saying they find the depth of coverage, relevance, and accuracy of the information found on *Wikipedia* to be *satisfactory* or *excellent*[36] . . . not too bad for a collection of information contributed and monitored by a self-selected army of unnamed and unknown volunteers. The key to *Wikipedia's* success in this area hinges upon the fact that those who are most qualified tend to edit and correct the postings of those who are not. This updating and revising of information continues ad infinitum until the *crowd* decides their work is done.

Think Different

Many of us will remember the Apple *think different* advertising campaign that suggested innovation was better when created by those willing to think in new and unique ways (i.e., Apple). In spite of the popularity of this promotion, research is revealing *thinking different* is only part of the equation . . . for better innovation and problem solving; we need to think different *together*.

Difference, or as we will hereafter call it *diversity*, is one of the key elements that enables crowdsourcing to be effective. For the purpose of our discussion, diversity means, "cognitive differences . . . differences in how

33. Page, *Difference*, xviii.
34. Terdiman, "Study: Wikipedia as Accurate as Britannica."
35. Ibid.
36. *Wikipedia*, "Nature Compares Wikipedia and Britannica," press release, Dec 15, 2005, https://en.wikipedia.org/wiki/Wikipedia:Press_releases/Nature_compares_Wikipedia_and_Britannica.

people see, categorize, understand, and go about improving the world."[37] Dr. Scott Page places these differences into four categories:[38]

> Diverse Perspectives: ways of representing situations and problems
>
> Diverse Interpretations: ways of categorizing or partitioning
>
> Diverse Heuristics: ways of generating solutions to problems
>
> Diverse Predictive Models: ways of inferring cause and effect[39]

People see the world in diverse ways. They organize what they see and experience in different cognitive categories. They approach problem solving in differing ways. And, they view the causes and effects of their decisions from different perspectives. Due to the diversity of these perspectives, almost everyone is advantaged over everyone else in some way due to the unique information they bring to the problem-solving table.[40]

A Diverse Toolbox

More than likely, each of us has some sort of toolbox at home. If we were to inventory the contents of this toolbox, we would be able to determine the types of projects these tools enable. In addition, we would be able to identify the area of someone's expertise by the quantity of tools that lend themselves to a particular specialty. The analogy of the toolbox is helpful as we consider our cognitive capabilities, since each of us also possess a variety tools in our cognitive toolboxes.[41]

Cognitive toolboxes help define us; they enable our capabilities and make obvious our limitations. "They determine how we do in school, how we play with others, the careers we choose, how much money we make, whether we are capable of having much fun, and how smart people think we are."[42] All things being equal, the more tools we carry around in our cognitive toolbox, the better able we are to successfully solve problems and

---

37. Page, *Difference*, xiv.
38. Ibid., 7.
39. Ibid.
40. Hayek, *Use of Knowledge in Society*, 521–22.
41. Page, *Difference*, 103.
42. Ibid., 104.

find creative solutions.[43] In light of this, some may fall victim to equating a vast cognitive toolbox with greater intelligence. However, the ability to find creative solutions has nothing to do with intelligence . . . at least not in the traditional ways in which we tend to measure IQ.

Understanding Intelligence

New understandings of intelligence are challenging the value we have traditionally placed on the IQ score as we are uncovering a variety of intelligences that render a single metric approach ineffective.

Dr. Howard Gardner has identified seven different types of intelligence:[44]

- Linguistic intelligence
- Musical intelligence
- Logical-Mathematical intelligence
- Spatial intelligence
- Bodily-Kinesthetic intelligence
- Intrapersonal intelligence
- Interpersonal intelligence

Psychologist Robert Sternberg approaches the topic from a slightly different perspective as a he attempts to explain intelligence through three distinct categories:[45]

- Analytic intelligence
- Creative intelligence
- Practical intelligence

Gardner and Sternberg's approaches are but two metrics available to us as a way to better understand the complicated topic of intelligence. However, irrespective of the way in which we approach the topic, there is one thing upon which we can agree: one needs a certain degree of intelligence to even begin to understand what we mean by intelligence.

---

43. Ibid., 105.
44. See Gardner, *Frames of Mind*.
45. See Sternberg, *Beyond IQ*.

Based upon what we do know about intelligence, we might be tempted to conclude gathering a group of *intelligent* individuals together in an attempt to solve difficult problems would be an appropriate strategy. However, this strategy comes with some rather counterintuitive words of caution.

Diversity Trumps Homogeneity

Most of us have heard the saying *great minds think alike*. While this phrase may effectively endear one person to others at a dinner party, thinking alike actually works to the disadvantage of effective problem solving. Research is showing "collections of people with diverse perspectives and heuristics outperform collections of people who rely on homogeneous perspectives and heuristics."[46] In other words, a group of individuals who do not share the same areas of "intelligence" outperform a collection of people who maintain the same or similar cognitive toolboxes.

C. S. Lewis once said: "Two heads are better than one, not because either is infallible, but because they are unlikely to go wrong in the same direction."[47] Going wrong in the same direction is more likely in a homogenous group of problem solvers because they share similar zones of *error blindness*[48] . . . zones in which something held to be true is actually false.[49] Homogeneous groups allow these error zones to remain invisible which limits potential outcomes. So, when working with a homogenous group of problem solvers, "two heads are not better than one in this case—they are one."[50]

Diversity Trumps Ability

If we find ourselves needing to solve a problem in an area in which we have no expertise, we might tend to seek out an authority or expert on the subject. For example, a leaky water pipe might encourage us to seek out a plumber while a car in need of alignment would prompt us to find an auto mechanic. These are effective and proper strategies when solving *simple*

---

46. Ibid., 10.
47. Lewis, *God in the Dock*, 202.
48. Schulz, *Being Wrong*, 18.
49. Ibid.
50. Page, *Difference*, 153.

problems. However, as the problems become more *complex*, the value an expert brings to the table tends to be overrated.[51]

Now, before anyone reading this attempts to justify the idea of consulting your friends at the gym as an effective way to diagnose your medical condition rather than consulting a team of experts on the matter, we should clarify: "a randomly selected collection of problem solvers outperforms a collection of the best individual problem solvers"[52] only under certain conditions.

Condition 1—The Problem Is Difficult[53]

If the problem were easy, there is a high likelihood several people in the group would individually know the answer. However, the benefits of diversity become apparent when we attempt to engage difficult problems such as designing products, curing disease, or improving our educational system.[54]

Condition 2—The Calculus Condition[55]

This condition states, "All of the possible problem solvers must have some ability to solve the problem."[56] In the case of your random selection of friends at the gym taking a stab at a diagnosis, we would assume this is the point at which they would be disqualified from participation.

Condition 3—The Diversity Condition[57]

This condition speaks to the differentiation between what is simply random, as compared to what is truly diverse. A random group has no better chance at arriving at a solution than would a group of "monkeys on typewriters trying to peck out a little Shakespeare."[58] Diversity, on the other hand, re-

---

51. Surowiecki, *Wisdom of Crowds*, 30.
52. Page, *Difference*, 162.
53. Ibid., 158.
54. Ibid., 159.
55. Ibid., 160.
56. Ibid., 159.
57. Ibid., 160.
58. Ibid.

quires the group of problem solvers be a collection of diverse individuals who can make an improvement or offer a valid contribution to the process. As such, no individual needs to be able to find the solution on his or her own, they just need to be able to offer a suggestion for improvement.[59]

Condition 4—Good-Sized Collections Drawn from Lots of Potential Problem Solvers[60]

This condition states the group working on a problem has to be bigger than a handful of individuals and drawn from a large population of potential problem solvers.[61] In other words: *two heads are better than one* is now better restated as *many heads are better than one or even a few*.

Diversity Trumps Polls

When discussing crowdsourcing, one of the questions that inevitably comes up is this: what is the difference between crowdsourcing and a poll? Poling is a method for checking the pulse of the general populace on a particular issue or a set of issues. It can be useful when investigating something with general interest to a large population group such as whether you prefer ketchup or salsa as a condiment or who is predicted to win an upcoming election. The randomness of a poll benefits this type of question.

However, when trying to solve a difficult problem, this randomness works against our ability to arrive at the best solution. The solving of a difficult problem requires a diverse set of problem-solving tools that a random selection process does not guarantee. Random is random and as such "the foolish and the wise alike get a single, equally weighted vote."[62]

Diverse Criteria

James Surowiecki, in his book *The Wisdom of Crowds*, proposes four conditions for what he calls wise crowds: "diversity of opinion (each person should have some private information, even if it's just an eccentric interpretation

---

59. Ibid., 161.
60. Ibid., 162.
61. Ibid.
62. Ibid., 161.

of the known facts), independence (people's opinions are not determined by the opinions of those around them), decentralization (people are able to specialize and draw on local knowledge), and aggregation (some mechanism exists for turning private judgments info a collective decision)."[63]

Diversity of Opinion

While the benefits of diversity have been discussed previously, it is important to include an additional criterion that encourages diversity in our problem-solving group: *we cannot select the members of the group*. When we select members for a group, we impose our personal bias upon the group thereby reducing diversity. In addition, if we are to participate in the problem-solving effort, we run the risk of our opinion exerting more influence than is warranted due to our position of privilege. A more effective strategy would be to allow members of the problem-solving community to self-select.

Self-selection may appear to place the problem-solving capabilities of a group at a disadvantage since those without adequate knowledge of the subject may choose to participate. However, as those within the group realize the lack of viable suggestions emanating from the unqualified, their influence within the group will decline to match their ability to contribute as good ideas rise to the top and bad ones sink to oblivion.

As an added benefit, research is also showing self-selection tends to encourage participation,[64] which seems to align with the enthusiasm exhibited by *Wikipedia's* self-selected volunteers.

Independence

Independence contributes to effective problem-solving in that independent problem solvers are less likely to be influenced by other members of the group through deliberation, which can reduce diversity by encouraging consensus.[65] Deliberation also contributes to groupthink, which can cause members of the problem-solving community to avoid controversy

---

63. Surowiecki, *Wisdom of Crowds*, 10.
64. Lakhani, *Principles of Distributed Innovation*, 105.
65. Howe, *Crowdsourcing*, 175.

or overlook weak arguments[66] thereby limiting the exploration of possibilities rather than creating a larger pallet of options from which to choose.[67] Therefore, keeping the participants independent of one another enables better problem solving and decision-making.

Decentralization

Decentralization has to do with leadership. When the decision group is decentralized, power and decision making is more likely to be shared or migrate toward those with independent knowledge of the situation as compared to power being held by an influential leader of the group.[68] Decentralization also tends to counter tendencies toward groupthink since it is harder for a decentralized group of individuals to influence one another's thoughts or actions.

Aggregation

Aggregation allows those who know the answer to reveal it[69] and those who know parts of the answer to contribute to the process of uncovering it.[70] Therefore, for a decentralized group to be able to generate intelligent results, there must be a means to aggregate everyone's input.[71] Fortunately, methods of aggregation are readily available on the Internet, which not only enable collaboration, but also make possible the hierarchical aggregation of potential solutions.

Monetizing Crowdsourcing

While crowdsourcing typically remains below the radar of those seeking solutions to ecclesiological challenges, corporate America is aggressively attempting to monetize crowdsourcing's benefits to create products and

---

66. Janis, *Groupthink and Group Dynamics*, 21.
67. Surowiecki, *Wisdom of Crowds*, 37.
68. Ibid., 70–71.
69. Page, *Difference*, 180.
70. Ibid.
71. Ibid., 74.

drive sales. To better understand how this is works, let's look at a few examples in the increasingly "crowded" marketplace.

Threadless is in the business of selling T-shirts; however, Threadless does not employ any T-shirt designers in the traditional sense. Instead, Threadless generates its designs from the efforts of a crowd of contributors who submit designs for consideration. Interestingly, the staff at Threadless is not determining which design is selected for production: that decision is made by a crowd of volunteers who visit the Threadless.com website to vote on their favorite designs. The designs that receive the highest number of votes are then manufactured and offered for sale with a percentage of the profits being returned to the designer. The crowd submits, the crowd votes and the crowd has the opportunity to affirm their decision with their cash by purchasing T-shirts.

iStockphoto.com is another example of a company marketing a crowdsourced inventory. Prior to iStockphoto, graphic design was historically a costly enterprise as most designs or photographs had to be created individually for specific client needs. In contrast to this model, iStockphoto encourages photographers, graphic designers and artists from all over the world to post their work in the iStockphoto database. Once their contribution is in the database, anyone looking for graphic images can scan the catalog in hopes of finding something that works for their particular application. At that point they can then license the image for a fraction of what it cost even a few years ago. Again, the licensing fee is split between iStockphoto and the creator of the image.

Quirky.com is another example of innovation being fueled via crowdsourcing in that Quirky allows inventors to submit designs or suggestions for new products to their website. I just glanced at the Quirky.com website and they have ideas posted for the following potential products: a note-taking smart pen, a heart-rate device that tells you your heart rate via your music player's headphones, a cereal bowl that prevents your cereal from getting soggy, and a thumbtack gun . . . to name a few.

Once an idea is submitted, Quirky lets people vote on the product or contribute ideas for its improvement. Ultimately, Quirky takes the best ideas (those with the highest number of votes) and not only manufactures them but markets them as well . . . of course while splitting the profits with the designer. A quick look at their current selection of products shows, among other things, something called the Pivot Power, which is basically a bendable power strip. The Quirky site says they have sold over six hundred thousand of these devices at a retail price of $29.95. The math would suggest, crowdsourcing works quite well for Quirky.com.

While we can see the benefits crowdsourcing brings to the table in a business or innovation context, how does this relate to the church and our ability to discern the voice of the Holy Spirit calling out to us today?

Spiritual Implications

Earlier, we attempted to understand the advantages diversity brings to problem solving through the metaphor of a toolbox. This metaphor can also be applied to the variety of ways in which we experience the Holy Spirit.

If we acknowledge that each of us brings a slightly different toolbox to that which life presents us, then it is logical to assume its influence extends into the ways in which we not only form our theologies, but also the ways in which we interpret those gentle nudging's of the Holy Spirit. In the midst of this interpretive stew, some of us will get it right, some of us will get it wrong, and some of us just won't get it at all. Therefore, anything that helps us identify and clarify the truth should be welcomed into our midst.

Embracing Innovation

Unfortunately, the church and innovation are not two words typically found in close *proximity* to one another. However, there have been times in which the church more readily embraced innovation as a way to better fulfill its calling. For an example of this, we need to rewind the hands of time about five hundred years and travel to Germany where a gentleman named Gutenberg reworked a wine press into something that made it easier to print. This innovation we know as the printing press, not only enabled Martin Luther's Reformation to spread across the countryside in unprecedented ways but also enabled those who had previously only heard the Bible read to them from the pulpit, to hold the Word in their hands for the very first time. Therefore, if the church were willing to embrace that same spirit of innovation in the area of crowdsourcing, we just might enable Luther's priesthood of believers to understand, discern, and respond to the voice of the Holy Spirit in ways never imagined.

Now I am not suggesting that crowdsourcing is the ultimate solution nor should it be the singular way in which we attempt to ascertain the voice of the Holy Spirit speaking to the church today. However, I am suggesting it is one way of heightening our listening skills . . . one tool in our toolbox . . . and as such, it deserves consideration.

Conclusion

In the book of Revelation, John describes a variety of visions in great detail. In these visions, we find one message repeated again and again as if to say . . . this is important, pay attention to this because it is something you all need to understand. The NRSV translates this text in the following way: "Let anyone who has an ear listen to what the Spirit is saying to the churches."[72]

The Message adds a little literary color to the text: "Are your ears awake? Listen. Listen to the Wind Words, the Spirit blowing through the churches."[73]

However you choose to read it, its meaning is clear. All of us, irrespective of our context, our calling, or our geography are called to turn our attention in the direction of the Wind Words . . . the Holy Spirit breeze that blows gently through our hearts; for when we do, we are instructed, corrected, and inspired to live in ways that glorify God . . . the source of those divine winds.

If you were a businessperson, the ways in which you might utilize crowdsourcing are fairly obvious. But, as a pastor or perhaps a person of influence within your church, how do you begin to take advantage of the benefits of crowdsourcing in your particular context?

First, do not diminish the voice of those on the fringes of your church, for the cognitive tools they bring to bear on the various issues facing your congregation may just locate them in a geography from which they can see the situation more clearly than yourself.

Second, encourage participation in the decisions that affect the church and the development of its mission strategies rather that attempting to enlist the congregation's participation in your particular vision of the future.

Third, be willing to test the waters of crowdsourcing by creating an online crowdsourcing presence from which you can engage your church in uncovering solutions to your particular challenges.

These are exciting times to be a follower of Jesus for we find ourselves facing opportunity no matter which way we turn. For those of us whose

---

72. Rev 2:7, 11, 17, 29; 3:6, 13, 22 NRSV.

73. Rev 2:7, 11, 17, 29; 3:6, 13, 22 *The Message*.

hearts are drawn toward care for the lost among us or for those of us whose primary attentions are better focused on the needs of the body, if we can heighten our ability to hear . . . to discern the voice of the Holy Spirit calling us to action, we will discover, we do indeed live in a world in which "every bush is burning."[74]

Bibliography

Dutton, William. "The Wisdom of Collaborative Network Organizations: Capturing the Value of Networked Individuals." *Prometheus* 26 (2008) 211–20.

Gardner, Howard. *Frames of Mind: The Theory of Multiple Intelligences*. New York: Basic, 2011.

Hall, Edward T. *The Hidden Dimension*. New York: Anchor, 1990.

Hayek, F. A. "The Use of Knowledge in Society." *American Economic Association* 35 (1945) 519–40.

Howe, Jeff. *Crowdsourcing: Why the Power of the Crowd Is Driving the Future of Business*. New York: Crown Business, 2008.

Janis, I. L. "Groupthink and Group Dynamics: A Social Psychological Analysis of Defective Policy Decisions." *Policy Studies Journal* 2 (1973) 19–25.

Lakhani, Karim R., and Jill A. Panetta. "The Principles of Distributed Innovation." *Innovations: Technology, Governance, Globalization* 2 (2007) 97–112.

Lewis, C. S. *God in the Dock: Essays on Theology and Ethics*. Grand Rapids: Eerdmans, 1994.

Page, Scott E. *The Difference: How the Power of Diversity Creates Better Groups, Firms, Schools, and Societies*. New ed. Princeton: Princeton University Press, 2008.

Schulz, Kathryn. *Being Wrong: Adventures in the Margin of Error*. Reprint. New York: Ecco, 2011.

Surowiecki, James. *The Wisdom of Crowds*. New York: Anchor, 2005.

Sternberg, Robert J. *Beyond IQ: A Triarchic Theory of Human Intelligence*. Cambridge: Cambridge University Press, 1985.

Sweet, Leonard. *Nudge: Awakening Each Other to the God Who's Already There*. Colorado Springs: Cook, 2010.

Terdiman, Daniel. "Study: Wikipedia as Accurate as Britannica." *CNET* (website). December 16, 2005. http://www.cnet.com/news/study-wikipedia-as-accurate-as-britannica.

---

74. Sweet, *Nudge*, 27.

8

Indefinable

Dan Kimball, DMin

I VERY DISTINCTLY REMEMBER being in Santa Fe, New Mexico, many years ago at a conference where Leonard Sweet was presenting. I had not previously heard of Len, this was my initial entry into the life and mind of this provocative man. As he took the stage and started speaking, I tried over and over to place him into a familiar category. I simply could not do it. There wasn't an available category or description for this speaker compared to all of the other Christian leaders that I was familiar with at the time.

He was a professor, but instead of being primarily concerned with offering a standard content dump of facts and information, he expanded our vision with numerous stories, metaphors, word pictures, and acronyms. To say it was spellbinding would not be an exercise in hyperbole.

His appearance did not even fit my experience of typical seminary professors. He was quite tall, with a J. Peterman-ish style, quite fashionable, yet not in a gaudy or trendy way. His voice was deep and like Leonard Cohen, and at times, was nearly hypnotic. His mind was that of an innovative, yet orthodox theologian. His storytelling transported us listeners into a visionary adventure. He was clearly learned, yet with an undeniable pastoral heart. He was truly unlike any other speaker I had previously listened to and I knew I wanted to learn more about his writings and who he was as a person.

I began by reading his book *Postmodern Pilgrims* that came at a critical moment for me. I was moving out of youth ministry at a megachurch with a very large high school ministry. However, I was staying in the church to launch a new college ministry since many teenagers were not connecting with the church as a whole. We had made many attempts to try and figure out ways to integrate high school students with the larger church, but nothing worked. I purposefully listened deeply to the students to try to understand exactly where they were coming from. It became that the impasse was not over theology. It surrounded how people experienced the ministry of the church. It was a disconnect of communication and learning styles, how we understood community and how we approached God in worship, and how we sought to win outsiders to faith in Jesus. This was all new to me and was rather puzzling. The church was not plateaued or declining, it was actually growing. But it was primarily connecting with middle-aged people. We were not at all connecting with younger people.

When I began reading *Postmodern Pilgrims*, it was clear that Len Sweet understood exactly what was happening. *Postmodern Pilgrims* was like reading a tour of current cultural developments and a missionary's explanation of how we might actually connect the gospel with this younger generation that we struggling to assimilate fully into our large church. Len had simply put in print exactly what I was experiencing but was clearly unable to articulate. We would not be able to simply change our music style to solve the problem; the root issues went much deeper.

Len simplified the core changes needed into the simple acronym EPIC (Experiential, Participatory, Image-Driven, and Connected.) This simple framing became part of my very ministry psyche. EPIC helped me to clearly explain to the church elders and staff that I was not alone in sensing what was really going on with young people.

I was personally thrilled to later write some of my own books and end up speaking at a conference with Len and to spend personal time with him. Whenever he was scheduled to make a presentation, I was genuinely excited to attend knowing that I was going to walk away with new insights into our changing culture and with plenty of fresh ideas of how to lead life-changing ministry with a new generation.

In one particular muggy, rainy weekend at a conference in New Hampshire, I listened to Len speak about the future of the Bible going digital and the changes it would create for all of us. This was way before smart phones or iPads or tablets, or Bible apps. Len described accurately what we all commonly experience today years before it happened.

Eventually, Len and I were scheduled to co-present together at a conference in San Diego. I have to admit, I felt like I a kindergarten student who was to share alongside their teacher in front of a large crowd. My heart was racing and I felt like I was about to experience a full-blown panic attack. Len came over and sat down next to me before the session began. With only a few gentle and encouraging words, my teacher was able to calm me down enough that I could confidently walk on stage with him. He had a unique way of making feel like a valued ministry peer and that we each had something worth sharing with others.

For those who have been to Len's home on Orcas Island, Washington, it is quite an amazing place. The home is filled with furniture, artwork, and even serving utensils from what looks like medieval times to the present. It is a home of stories. Each lighting fixture or doorknob has some particular meaning from some specific place of origin.

Len's study (the Star Chamber) is a tightly packed library, complete with a writing desk, art, sculptures, and multiple decorative pipes hanging in various racks. One is overcome with the feeling that all kinds of possibilities will be birthed in that room.

On one particular night in the Star Chamber, I was in desperate need of some advice. Len sat high on a carved antique chair as I began to share with him some of my struggles. I recounted my struggle and hurt as several of my ministry friends were heading down theological paths that I simply could not follow. Len listened intently and gently kept bringing me back to church history and the clear patterns of the past. It felt like I was opening a history of theology book and listening to the saints of old share about what had gone before and yet in a manner that was surprisingly relevant in the twenty-first century.

More than anything else, I remember that Len kept bringing it all back to Jesus. Not the pop-American Jesus, or the Jesus of a specific denomination, or the Jesus that is stuck on to the latest ministry trends. But the historical, biblically rooted Jesus, the one who inspired the gospel writers. This Jesus calmed me and yet also gave me the inspired confidence to make some decisions that I simply had to make. That was the night where I learned to deeply appreciate biblical and church history. I listened to how God worked in the past to understand how he was leading me into the future.

In all my interactions with Len, Jesus has always been the center of all of our discussions. When I consider what I have truly learned from him, it isn't simply futuristic thinking, or ministry methodology, or even the importance of EPIC approaches. But what you walk away from considering all of his metaphors and analogies you end with Jesus as the center of everything. As much as I can appreciate Len's scholarship and creative thinking, what stands out the most to me is his love for Jesus.

I still cannot define Len Sweet as a thinker, writer, speaker, or even as a man according to any clearly defined category. But what rubs off on me from Len is his humble yet confident trust in Jesus. To think futuristically is to truly meditate on Jesus past, present and future. To love and care for the church and explore needed ministry methods is to never forget that Jesus is the head of the church and not all of our fancy ideas and the fads of the month.

His greatest lesson as my teacher is that we must never stray from proper humility and genuine awe of the One we serve and worship.

> The Son is the image of the invisible God, the firstborn over all creation. For in him all things were created: things in heaven and on earth, visible and invisible, whether thrones or powers or rulers or authorities; all things have been created through him and for him. He is before all things, and in him all things hold together. And he is the head of the body, the church; he is the beginning and the firstborn from among the dead, so that in everything he might have the supremacy. For God was pleased to have all his fullness dwell in him, and through him to reconcile to himself all things, whether things on earth or things in heaven, by making peace through his blood, shed on the cross.[1]

When I think about this passage, I think about Len's life and message—all of our ministry approaches and efforts are nothing without Christ. We are not meant to be *about* Christ, but *with* Christ and *for* Christ.

Yes, Len has offered church leaders some helpful metaphors to better understand how to do what we are called to do. Yes, Len has proven to be startling accurate at times in how our culture's future will unfold among us. Yes, Len has a passion for the church to effectively engage in mission in an ever-changing world. But when I personally consider my mentor and friend, it is that it is Jesus who has created all things and that in him all things hold together. It is Jesus who is the is the head of the body, the church, that we all serve and think about at conferences and in the ministry books that we write and read.

Len's unique mixture of various roles as scholar, pastor, leader, professor, writer, communicator, historian, futurist, and historian truly make him indefinable. But what is definable is his consistent pointing to the supremacy of Jesus. This is the one definable trait of the indefinable Leonard Sweet.

---

1. Col 1:15–20 NIV.

9

Identity, Vocation and Calling

David McDonald, DMin

> The only way to access the universal is through the particular.
>
> —*Leonard Sweet*[1]

I'M NOT SURE WHAT words and images come to your mind when you hear the name Leonard Sweet. I thought of Len as a diviner and a sage and a hero.

Then, when I met him, I realized Len was something else entirely.

In the early 2000s I was working as a college pastor and struggling to make sense of the massive cultural shift we were experiencing in our church. The dominant ministerial paradigms focused on attraction and replication both at home and overseas. But they weren't making sense any longer, and the old ministries were no longer bearing fruit. The byline of church prophets and strategists alike was that "boomer" churches would have to adapt in order to reach "Gen Xers."

But I was dissatisfied with that answer.

I was the poster child for Gen X-rated Christianity, except I was almost ten years too young to be considered part of that demographic. I knew these so-called "generational" shifts were only the early warning signs of a

---

1. Leonard Sweet, in discussion with the author, June 2010.

more significant change. Len helped me identify that change, in his book *SoulTsunami*,[2] as the shift from modernity to postmodernity.

And that changed everything.

Here was a guy totally disinterested in the next big ministry trend or the next version of cool church. This was someone who wanted to know where the culture was headed, and to head it off at the pass.

> The only way to hit a moving target is to get in front of it.
>
> —Leonard Sweet[3]

I hounded Len from a distance for several years—reading all his books and eavesdropping on him at conferences—but I only met him when I enrolled in the Doctor of Ministry program at the George Fox Evangelical Seminary. My opinion of him as the postmodern Jesus-Yoda only intensified, until I finally mustered the courage to call him up and ask him for advice about the ministry at our church.

That was when my bubble burst.

At the time, our church[4] was doing a series on creation and evolution. My take was that—even if evolution were proven to be entirely accurate—the authority of the Scripture was unmarred. But no matter what I said in public, I kept receiving accusations that I was an evolutionist who refused to take the Bible authoritatively.

I called Len and asked for his advice about how to get people off my back. Do you know what he said?

"Don't waste your time."

"What do you mean"? I asked.

"Evolution isn't your thing," he replied. "Your job is to do what God has put in you to do. Did he call you to win the war on Intelligent Design?"

"No," I replied.

"What then?"

"I want to change the church. I want to translate the gospel into the language of twenty-first-century pop culture, the *koine* of the contemporary world."

---

2. *SoulTsunami* contains Len's call for a postmodern missiology rather than an ecclesiological set against the massive cultural shift away from modernism.

3. Waddle, "Q&A: Reality TV."

4. Westwinds Community Church, where I currently serve as teaching pastor (www.westwinds.org).

"So do that," he replied.

And hung up.[5]

That was the moment I realized Len was more sensei than sage. He has the impatience of a prophet, but the heart of a poet. He delights in creating his own complexity, but ruthlessly slashes the extraneous bits of self-doubt, anxiety, and masturbatorial agenda-keeping that make the church impotent, flaccid, and pale.

I'm going to show you how I've applied Len's theories to real-life ministerial practice. By necessity I will rely heavily on personal anecdotes, but I feel confident that when you read about how we've parsed this material into actual ministry you'll be encouraged that you can do the same.

I've also included a couple of diagrams I use to translate Len's thinking into action.[6] There is a danger that the diagrams will feel formulaic. They shouldn't. Using these diagrams won't guarantee similar results, just a similar process.

We'll begin by exploring what Len has taught me about myself (and by extension, *you*, the reader), and then explore Len's understanding of the people I've been called to serve (and by extension, *them*, the people you're called to serve), and finally Len's teaching on the place where I minister, Jackson, Michigan (and by extension, *there*, the place where you serve).

YOU

You can't be anyone but yourself. At best you might become a B+ imitation, but the people around you will always feel like you're sporting a facade.

Because you are.

Len taught me to figure out who I was by citing an old rabbinical legend about Rabbi Zusya, a Chasidic master who lived in the eighteenth century. He's famous for saying, "When I get to the heavenly court, God will not ask me, 'Why weren't you Moses?' Rather he will ask me, 'Why were you not Zusya?'"

One of Len's major complaints with the church at large is that we're all trying to be someone we're not. We've bought into the modern

---

5. Leonard Sweet, in discussion with the author, September 2008. Though the conversation was longer, I wrote Len's words down verbatim at the time.

6. This is the first time I've shared these with anyone. They are sketches I've drawn in my personal journals, for personal use, to try to figure out how to apply Len's teaching. Ironically, he hates this kind of thing—it's too linear.

manufacturing paradigm that says B + C = A, so if we can just discover the formula for creating *Better* programs and *Creative* churches, we'll ensure *A+* pastors.

But it doesn't work like that.

The more you try to pretend you're the next Billy Sunday, Bono, or Henri Nouwen, the more you give yourself permission to act like the world owes you the respect it never gave them. Thus the B + C prescription produces fewer A-postles than A-holes.

> Life is false to formula.
>
> —*Leonard Sweet*[7]

Reducing the complexity of personal calling and vocation to a repeatable process incubates mediocrity (at best), if not total missional misconduct.[8]

The truth is that God has summoned us to lead.[9] We have been "called into existence by circumstance."[10] Like Esther we have been placed here, now, for this. And the harder we work to be like Rick Warren or Billy Graham or Leonard Sweet, the further we travel from the purposes and plans of God.

That doesn't mean we can't learn from one another. But the avenues for education and enrichment are the means, not the ends. We learn more by understanding Rick Warren's thought process than by simply copying Saddleback's church services. If we follow recklessly after God like they do, the manifestation of God's Spirit will be equally intense in us.

Don't look for replication, but innovation.

Don't try for implementation, but imagination.

Don't model procedures, but creativity.

For the record, being creative isn't easy. "Innovation inspires a culture of complaint,"[11] but you've got to do what God has put in you to do, and grow skin thick enough to do it well for a long time.

---

7. Sweet, *Summoned to Lead*, 179.
8. Sweet, *Aqua Church*, 18.
9. See Sweet, *Summoned to Lead*.
10. Ibid., 12.
11. Sweet, *So Beautiful*, 216.

Len once told me about a group of pastors during the Roman persecution. Since churches often held their gatherings in crypts, many pastors were employed as gravediggers. It was the perfect cover. They dug out huge cave systems and gallerias, some of which spanned hundreds of acres and descended more than four stories underground. Their familiarity with the tomb-ways allowed them to select the best possible venues for Christian worship.

One key facet of their subterranean piety was the beautification of those catacombs with Christian symbols, scriptures, and prayers.

There is a kind of insect that lives underground and lays its eggs in the sand. It is from these insects that the gravedigger priests took their name: Fossores.[12] So, too, those pastors were laying the eggs of the future church in the sands of the crypts of Rome.

Len challenged me to become a "Fossorian," someone for whom there was an unbroken wholeness between art, work, and faith.

I began to ask myself some very basic questions. Previously, I had been so focused on what God wanted me to do that I had neglected who God wanted me to become. Please understand I knew God wanted me to be holy, to be like him, to be devoted, to be passionate, to constantly be learning and growing and developing, etc. But—specifically—I didn't have a good answer to the question "What does the best possible version of David McDonald look like?"

The more I prayed and sought the face of God, the more the answers startled me. I never expected God to authenticate my love of science fiction, for example, since everyone else in my life had always cautioned me against old wives' tales. Neither did I anticipate that God would help me find meaning in hagiographies and patristic folklore. These discoveries energized the fantastical components of my imagination, encouraging a sci-fi crossover with classical theology.

My investigation into fossorian spirituality began with *The UnDwellable City*,[13] a series of science fiction novels I wrote for my son. At the time, Jacob was distressingly bored by church and came home miserable every Sunday. We had great family devotionals, and he prayed regularly on his own, but church was a chore. To help, I asked him what could make church better. He didn't know. After weeks of gently pulling information out of him, I tried another tactic and asked Jacob about his five favorite things

---

12. Hassett, "Fossors."
13. See www.TheUnDwellableCity.org.

in the world. He told me they were scuba diving, sports, adventure stories, Atlantis, and zombies.

I took those five things and called together some of the people at our church—an artist, a graphic designer, a teacher, and a media presenter. I told them I was going to write a science fiction "gospel" for my son and would like their help to turn it into an after-school mid-year VBS, a live storytelling experience, and five illustrated novels. No one had ever done anything like this before, but we tried and it was a smash success. The novels were released one-a-month through the church. They told the story of a Sunday School teacher traveling to Atlantis on the anniversary of his wife's death. After all five books had been released, we held our after-school program and nearly every child that attended came from the local elementary schools (i.e., they were not church kids) to hear the story told in small chunks and learn about Christology while playing with Legos. The kids built submarines and sea monsters with toy bricks, then acted out their favorite parts of the story in groups. At the conclusion of the VBS, we invited the kids, their families, our church, and the community to a live storytelling experience in a large performing arts theater. I stood up and told a one hundred thousand–word novel in ninety minutes, received a standing ovation, and gave all the proceeds to a local charity that focuses on literacy.

That was the first time I felt like a Fossorian. My art (literature), my work (pastoral leadership) and my faith (as a father and as a speculative theologian) had joined together precisely as Len admonished.

I have done other storytelling projects—most recently *The Revelation of June Paul*,[14] which offered a counter-proposal to *Left Behind* dispensationalism and a counterpoint to the Rolling Stones' *Sympathy for the Devil*—but *The UnDwellable City* was the first and the most personal.

I was aware, however, that I had only experienced this "unbroken wholeness" outside of the confines of my normal, everyday life. The stories were great but they were special projects. I wanted my entire waking life to feel that kind of synergism, and I still had a long way to go.

Part of the problem was my perspective on church leadership. As a whole, Western Christians tend to view ministry as a kind of sacred management. Secular leadership thinking governs how we do what we do, with some scripture stapled to a few ideas so they feel godly.

This is a major problem, and something we must ultimately curb.

---

14. See www.TheRevelationOfJunePaul.com.

The definitive moment came for me when a publisher called and asked me to write something on leadership, and I didn't want to. I realized then that if I was going to give my life to something, I didn't want it to be "helping people lead"; I wanted it to be "helping people feel saturated with the Spirit." But when I pitched that idea to the publisher they told me no one would be interested. To be fair, this particular publisher dealt predominantly with leadership material, but it felt strange that leadership and spirituality should be divorced.

I wanted to bring them back together in my own life. And if I couldn't, then it was clear "leadership" had to go.

> As the business world sees the leader's role as rearranging reality and filtering facts into iconic symbols of healing and redemption, how much more should the church be very clear about its mission of healing and redemption.
>
> —Leonard Sweet[15]

Len has always banged the drum in opposition to the church's leadership infatuation. He reminds us we are followers first and any "leadership" is really "followership" ("follow me as I follow Christ"[16]).[17] Because of his repeated emphasis on the creation narratives of Genesis 1 and 2, every time I heard Len speak I began to wonder what it was like for Adam to be the first follower. He was called to "conserve and conceive God's creativity,"[18] and he derived his vocation directly from his identity as an image-bearer of the Almighty.

Looking deeper into *tselem* (the Hebrew word for "image") I realized it has a wide range of meanings. It can mean "image," or "copy," or "idol" (that's the best translation, actually) or "shadow." I've always found the "image-bearer" language very angular. Normal people can't use "image-bearer" in a sentence while drinking coffee at Starbucks, not unless they're taking a philosophy class and have a penchant for speaking in British raj or wearing black berets. I began playing with the alternative renderings of *tselem*, certain there was an important clue hidden there to help me speak about the inherent spirituality of following God while doing God's work

---

15. Sweet, *Summoned to Lead*, 111.
16. See 1 Cor 11:1.
17. See Sweet, *I Am a Follower*.
18. Sweet, *Jesus: A Theography*, 42.

for (and with) others. I found myself coming back again and again to the word "shadow."

That's who we really are: shadows of God. We go where God goes. We do what God does. We're *like* him. Shadowing God requires that we stay in step with God's activity and movement in the world. Shadowing God requires that we love what God loves and recognize that we have no real control over what he does or where he goes. Our only job is to stay with him so the shadow doesn't get distorted.

This, then, became my way of talking about church leadership and of spirituality in general. In fact, it's the way our entire church now talks about being human. We're shadowing God—whether as leaders, or first followers, or ministers, or plumbers, or business people, or stay-at-home moms.

It's become such an inherent part of our church fabric that we don't even use the word "leader." Our people just refer to the areas they lead as one way they're "shadowing God." They don't see it as a special privilege; they just feel like it's a normal part of life. God has moved them to a place where they need to lead in order to stay in step with his Spirit.

The following diagram is a little exercise I developed to figure out what I should do with my time and energy based on my passion, my vocation, and my identity. The shapes outside the Venn diagram that enclose the exclamation marks are reminders about why the intersection of any two of these three areas is insufficient and will leave you wanting more.

I suggest you use this diagram to process your own thoughts about who you are, what you can do, and what you love. Feel free to scribble all over it, use it and reuse it, changing it as often or as oddly as necessary.

FINDING YOUR HOLY #CALLING:
letting what you do flow from who you are

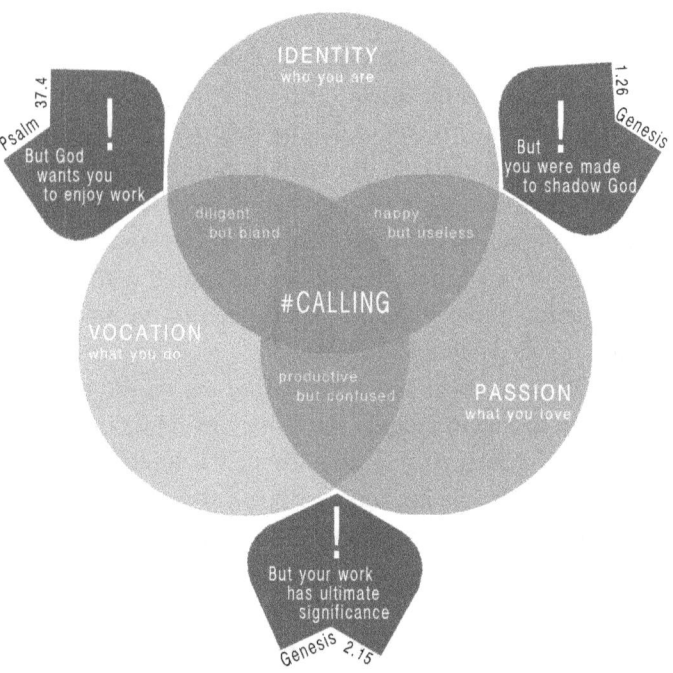

Them

Len loves to challenge conventional wisdom. If "everyone" is saying the same thing, he figures we've got a blind spot and wants to shed some light on the underexposed corners of our assumptions.

Case in point, Len hates the phrase "God's plan."

I'm not sure there's a more destructive idea out there, with less biblical support, than the idea that God has just one plan for your life—just one woman you could marry, just one career, just one mission—and if you mess it up, you're outside his will.[19]

In *Summoned to Lead*, Len clarifies that instead of telling people "God has a plan" for them (and the necessary misquoting of Jeremiah), we should tell them they "are part of God's larger purposes and design" for the world.[20]

And what is God's larger purpose?

To heal the world.

God made creation inherently good.[21] But that goodness has been corrupted.[22] He plans to come back and make it good again.[23] Our task is to cooperate with God as he works to heal the world. We're agents of reconciliation,[24] called to steward the earth[25] and to celebrate those moments where the kingdom of God already looks to be breaking into the kingdom of this world,[26] replacing sorrow with joy.[27]

Every Christian is part of God's long-term plan to heal the world. Any "healing" with which we can help—economic, emotional, cultural, physical, ecological—"counts" as part of God's mission.

Our people at Westwinds love this idea because it gives them the freedom to come up with new ways to be faithful. They might not be able to confidently go door-to-door to hand out tracts, but knowing that any healing activity is important to God has spurred them to renovate neighbors' bathrooms, clean up the local river, visit the elderly in care homes, prepare meals for new mothers, etc. "Healing the world" is a compelling metanarrative, and it has allowed our people innumerable ways to shadow God.

We've got to stop telling people what to do and what to think. If, instead, we can help them figure out their role in the story of God, then the momentum of the Spirit will naturally guide their actions and thoughts toward a finale. Good thoughts and actions will take us closer to the finale.

---

19. Leonard Sweet and Chuck Conniry, in discussion with the author, March 2013.
20. Sweet, *Summoned to Lead*, 106.
21. Gen 1:4, 10, 12, 18, 21, 25.
22. Rom 5:12–21.
23. Isa 65:17–25.
24. 2 Cor 5:11–21.
25. Gen 1:28.
26. Mark 1:15.
27. Matt 5:3–10.

And the power of that story will help people decide for themselves which thoughts and actions they want to cultivate.

> We can no longer afford to expect thinking to be a function of those at the top and doing a function of those at the bottom. None of us is as smart as all of us.
>
> —*Leonard Sweet*[28]

Our role as shepherds has little to do with shepherding the health and well-being of our people (after all, most of our people are healthier than we are anyway—they don't have to eat all the baked goods they bring to the church office), and much more to do with shepherding their dreams and noble ambitions.

I remember asking Len once about some discipleship material. At the time, our people were very excited about Beth Moore's highly successful Bible studies and Rick Warren's wildly popular *Purpose Driven Life*. We didn't offer classes on either of these books and were getting some pressure to do so. Len's response made me immediately regret my willingness to capitulate.

"No—absolutely don't do that," he said.

"Why not?"

He sighed. "Because it's not in *you*."

"But it'll grow the church."

"Of course. It's good material. But you're not trying to grow the church. You're trying to grow your people. And if they're going to be healthy, you need to feed them home-cooked meals."[29]

That conversation reminded me that my task isn't to grow the church's platform but to use the church as a platform for our people to shadow God and heal the world.

The church is at her best when she functions like YouTube. Everyone gets to "upload" their stories about healing the world. The church provides scaffolding and outlines basic codes of conduct, but the people are released to shadow God in whatever way seems best.

---

28. Sweet, *Summoned to Lead*, 108.
29. Leonard Sweet and John Voelz, in discussion with the author, March 2010.

To assist further, we developed our "Beyond 1000"[30] initiative designed to help us become a G.O.O.D.[31] church. Every quarter we award each department in our church (youth, kids, media) a thousand-dollar grant to invest in the community. They're required to come up with a plan that wins a triple bottom line of investing one thousand dollars, earning back another one thousand dollars to reinvest, and getting press coverage for the event. Some of our Beyond 1000 initiatives have included art fairs, car repair days, home renovations for under-resourced families, folk music festivals, free stores, poetry contests, after-school programs, and a zombie walk (that one was my favorite).

But all this activity necessitated finding a way to differentiate between charity and mission, since our people were growing very comfortable with doing good deeds but increasingly uncomfortable mentioning Jesus to the people they served. We introduced a matrix we call our Kingdom Quotient to keep everyone's attention focused on Christ. Now we coach them that every single thing we do needs to ensure the name of Jesus is elevated, that our church needs to be included as part of the story, that we need to understand the biblical foundations for why we do what we do, and that we need to invite the Spirit to change us as we do it.

For example, when our people want to pass out baked goods at the InterFaith shelter, we tell them it's a fantastic idea. Then we do a little role-playing with them so they get comfortable saying the name of Jesus in conversation without it feeling forced or overly religious. (It's a lot more fun to say, "I love Jesus, and he loves baking, so these are for you . . . ," than it is to say, "I am doing this because I am a follower of Jesus Christ who, despite living a long time ago in a very distant location, still would approve of this seemingly random act of kindness in his name. Amen.") We might take them through a short Bible study, anchoring their noble deeds in the New Testament (Eph 2:10, for example, talks about God preparing good works for us to do). We remind them to have some Westwinds literature or invitation cards handy, just so people can connect the dots. We didn't always value that, actually, but our church is so full of wonderful weirdos that people in our small town began imagining we were a cult. By connecting our church name with our good works, the community impression changed from "young punks with tattoos" to "punks who do what Jesus told

---

30. Our church address is 1000 Robinson Road, so "beyond 1000" refers to our desire to move past our property markers and into the community.

31. Reis, "Do You Trust the Story?"

them to." Finally, we encourage all our participants to stay prayerful during the ministry time and have them invite the Spirit to change their hearts as they serve. Service is no guarantee of transformation—hence the proliferation of sour nuns and angry missionaries—so we need to be mindful that we don't burn out or take God's transforming power for granted. We tell our people they need to regularly ask God: "What are you saying to me?" and "What do you want me to do?"

The following diagram is adapted from a floor-to-ceiling illustration in our offices. We use it during our planning sessions for any major missional initiative.

There

Where you are matters as much as who you are.

It's no good thinking through your identity and vocation if you cannot make it work at home. What works in New York City won't work in Saskatoon. Your time and place matter, and "the incarnation is the intersection of the timeless with time."[32]

32. T. S. Eliot, as quoted in Sweet, *So Beautiful*, 162.

Len says, "Jesus' disciples are like water," meaning we can "take the shape of everything without losing the essence of who we are."[33] That's good news. It means that we can all find ways to make ministry work at home, even if "home" is a foreign country, the wrong side of the tracks, or someplace other than our secret fantasy congregation on the beach.

A pig farmer, submitted to God and cooperating with the Spirit, can be incarnated in downtown Chicago, just as a railroad tycoon can find some way to heal the world on an island in the Caribbean. The only requirement is that they pay attention to where God has placed them and not fight against it.

To start with, you're going to have to make some things up. By this, I mean you and your people cannot simply take someone else's program, curriculum, emphasis, or slogan. Nope. Our task involves doing the hard work of parsing the gospel for our context.

But, you might ask, what about all the amazing stuff available for dirt-cheap from our denominational publisher? Or the fabulous free stuff from the latest mega-sexy-Jesus-fad conference? Isn't that so much better than anything we could do ourselves?

Maybe.

Maybe that's one way to look at it.

Another way to look at it involves thinking about whether it's better to create new life with your spouse or buy a baby off the Internet. Sure, making your own baby takes longer and there are some risks. Your offspring, after all, might have the same lisp you do or the same waddle . . . but what kind of creepy pervert would buy a baby?

I'm overstating.

A little.

But ministry flows out of *you*, not them.

Some of you might disagree. You might consider using someone else's material akin to adoption. But adoption is usually more costly than natural childbirth, not less. And even in those cases where adoption is the only option for people to begin a family, they explore the process having exhausted all other avenues. Furthermore, adoption is a relationship. It's one thing to foster Christ-like relationships—reaching out to those less fortunate with love—but quite another thing to adopt a program.

Too many churches don't even seem willing to try to conceive. We've forgotten that making the baby is part of the fun, blithely resolving that it's

---

33. Sweet, *So Beautiful*, 183.

too hard to make our own and we should buy someone else's instead. But if you just nab things others have created for people in their church, your ministry will never quite fit into your context. At best you're the out-of-place adult wearing a concert T-shirt at the Miley Cyrus show; at worst, you're guilty of buying babies.

Adoption is noble. Copying someone else's ministry idea is just lazy.

God hasn't called you to copy others. God has called you to minister to your people with the gifts he's given you. Don't take shortcuts. Don't cheat. Bleed your own blood. "Franchise is another word for dis-incarnation."[34]

In *So Beautiful*,[35] Len lists three requirements for incarnational innovation. First, everyone needs a high contextual intelligence, meaning you've got to "get" your city, your town, or your neighborhood. Learn what makes the people tick, what they value, and what they fear.

Second, everyone needs to understand that—even in the right location—the right idea requires the right timing. No one comes to a nativity in the summer.

Finally, everyone needs to understand that—while structures matter—the specific form and shape of any endeavor comes from its essence. Consider that every coffee shop has comfortable chairs and side tables so you can happily drink coffee and talk with friends; or consider that every bookstore is well lit and patrons are encouraged to leaf through books and happily experience the leisure of reading right there, right away.

The way we do things must match up with the things themselves. There's no point in hosting a cake walk during the season finale of *The Biggest Loser*.

One of the ways you can begin to determine the pulse of your community is to look for the dominant cultural symbols and figure out what's going on behind them. Our town, for example, has a huge underground folk music audience. Music is a powerful symbol in its own right, but my co-pastor began to realize there was something deeper behind the music of southern Michiganders. He realized they were yearning for redemption.

Jvo took things a step further and began playing in a folk trio that toured around the state.[36] Whenever he played, people would come up to him (usually drunk or stoned) and talk about their own need for forgiveness, or restoration, or healing (either social or relational). Jvo was inun-

---

34. Ibid., 158.
35. Ibid., 201–2.
36. See Voelz, *Quirky Leadership*.

dated with bad news—with un-gospel, so to speak—and began formulating a plan to tell good news instead. He started a folk festival called FolkGalore and invited a bunch of bands from around the state to come together under the banner of: *Music. Story. Redemption.* In so doing he was able to offer good news in a way that made sense to our community. Sometimes he was able to share the gospel implicitly through music, but many times he was able to share the gospel explicitly through words because of the connections he made through his music.

If you were to analyze Jvo's approach, you'd see that he first identified a powerful cultural symbol (folk music) and then the value behind it (redemption), before retelling the story of our people using their own symbols and offering up Jesus as the ultimate fulfillment of their search for redemption.

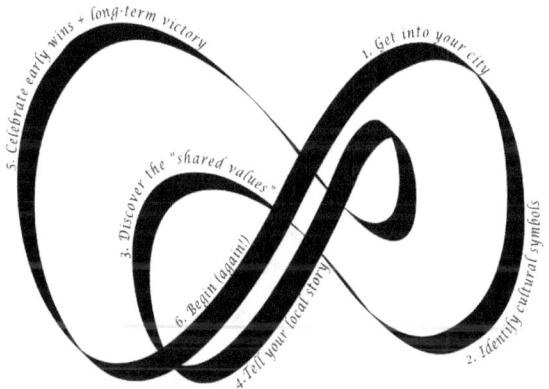

Conclusion

I began this chapter by rehearsing a conversation I had with Len that reframed my ministry. Let me now conclude with another, equally poignant, phone call.

While trying to untangle the mess of Len Sweet-isms in one of the fifty-two books he wrote in 2008 (give or take—I may have rounded up), I began to despair.

"I can't keep it all straight," I complained.

"David," he replied, "just remember: the only way to navigate complexity is with simplicity."

That stuck with me. It's possible to think some things to death, to get so caught up in trying to do things right that what you actually do is a convoluted mess. So, after all I've said in this chapter to try to parse Len's teaching in real life, let me sum up what he's taught in the simplest way possible:

God has called *you here* to help *them now*.

Why would you ever do anything else?

Bibliography

Hassett, Maurice. "Fossors." In *The Catholic Encyclopedia*. New York: Appleton, 1909. Available at New Advent, http://www.newadvent.org/cathen/06155a.htm.

McDonald, David. *The Revelation of June Paul*. Jackson, MI: Westwinds Church, 2012.

———. *The UnDwellable City*. Colorado Springs: Samizdat, 2011.

Reis, Andrew. "Do You Trust the Story? A Weekend with Leonard Sweet." *Spectrum* (magazine), April 3, 2012. http://spectrummagazine.org/node/3898.

Sweet, Leonard. *Aqua Church*. Loveland, CO: Group, 1999.

———. *I Am a Follower: The Way, the Truth, and the Life of Following Jesus*. Nashville: Nelson, 2012.

———. *So Beautiful: Divine Design for Life and the Church*. Colorado Springs: Cook, 2009.

———. *SoulTsunami*. Grand Rapids: Zondervan, 1999.

———. *Summoned to Lead*. Grand Rapids: Zondervan, 2004.

Sweet, Leonard, and Frank Viola. *Jesus: A Theography*. Nashville: Nelson, 2012.

Voelz, John. *Quirky Leadership*. Nashville: Abingdon, 2013.

Waddle, Ray. "Q&A: Reality TV Can Teach Us about Relationships." UMC.org. http://archives.umc.org/interior.asp?mid=1367.

10

Rearranging the Furniture of Faith

Mike McNichols, DMin

> The essential destination of Christianity isn't *what* but *who*. Being in the household of faith means having a relationship with God through Jesus the Christ as revealed in the Scriptures. The furniture of faith is the creeds, the confessions, the doctrines, and the articles of religion that have been handed down to us by our ancestors.
>
> —*Leonard Sweet*[1]

EVERY SO OFTEN, IN the household of faith, the furniture gets moved around.[2]

When I was young, my mother used to rearrange our furniture on a regular basis. It was always fun to experience the change, but a bit disorienting at first. My dad, my brother, and I would come home from work or school to a house where our internal navigation devices had to be reset to accommodate the relocation of chairs, couches, and tables. Even our dog would take a while to get used to the changes.

But it was still our home, and we continued to be together. Regardless of the shift in furnishings, we didn't let go of our common identity. In the midst of rethinking the way we expressed our shared life through physical,

---

1. *Out of the Question . . . Into the Mystery*, 29.

2. As Phyllis Tickle observes, "Every five hundred years, give or take a decade or two, Western culture . . . goes through a time of enormous upheaval, a time in which essentially every part of it is reconfigured" (*Emergence Christianity*, 17).

tangible accouterments, we seemed to be able to hold on to the essence of what it meant to be a family.

There are significant forces causing the furniture of creeds, confessions, doctrines, and articles of religion to be challenged, shifted, and sometimes even discarded. Those forces come from both inside and outside the church, resulting in new—and sometimes disorienting—issues and questions. Regardless of one's faith tradition, the church is being confronted with challenges such as:

> *The redefining of marriage.* What, then, does it mean to be human—to be male and female, male or female, made in the image of God?[3] What authority regarding marital relationships—if any—can be found in our Scriptures? What is the church's relationship to the state, as they continue to cooperate together in the legalization of a marriage?

> *Immigration reform.* Do national boundaries trump relationships in the body of Christ?[4] Are our neighbors only those who share a common citizenship? Do I encounter a hungry, thirsty, cold Jesus only in the faces of those who wave my nation's flag?

> *Bioethics.* If a child's life begins in a laboratory, is she endowed with a God-imaged humanity? When a pregnancy is medically terminated, do we label the process a reasonable act of choice, or is it the killing of a future person? Because something *can* be done through medical technology, *should* it be done?

> *Internet technology and virtual reality.* Are these technologies moving us from a text-based culture to an image-based culture?[5] If so, what will be the effect on followers of Jesus who have, for centuries, relied on written texts of Scripture to define faith,

---

3. In reference to Karl Barth, Ray Anderson speaks of "ordered ontology": "By 'ordered ontology' I mean that every human has an essential created structure that is sexually and personally differentiated, as male and female, male or female" (*Shape of Practical Theology*, 274).

4. "So then you are no longer strangers and aliens, but you are citizens with the saints and also members of the household of God, built upon the foundation of the apostles and prophets, with Christ Jesus himself as the cornerstone" (Eph 2:19–20 NRSV).

5. See Rosen, *Image Culture*.

ethics, and community? Are relationships being enhanced or damaged by the Internet? What does it mean to be together?[6]

The disruption of Christendom. As Western culture continues to challenge Christianity as a dominant narrative, will the church critique itself or fight to reclaim its perceived cultural power? Will our Western social imaginaries[7] be formed by the work of God's Spirit, by the power of consumerism, or by other societal and cultural forces? Will the church revisit its interpretations of its own story and discard the hubris that claims we have everything right? Can we have new conversations and find fresh theological metaphors without discarding our Scriptures?

These are not issues and questions that live only in the academy. Many pastors have conversations about these topics with congregants who are trying to sort out relationships with their gay loved ones, or who are trying to prevent the deportation of an undocumented worker whose family will be devastated by the loss, or who are anguishing over whether to allow their fifteen-year-old daughter to terminate her pregnancy.

Pastors and Christian leaders rarely operate in the abstract. They minister in a world that is tragically and painfully real. And as the furniture continues to be moved around, they have to deal with some very real questions, such as:

- What does it mean, in this time and place, to be the people of God?
- What is the nature of the church in the world?
- In the midst of social and ecclesial earthquakes, will the church be capable of some form of unity that becomes the answer to Jesus' prayer, "That they may all be one . . . so that the world may believe that you have sent me"?[8]

---

6. Margaret Wheatley considers this to be an important question: "I believe the fundamental work of this time—work that requires the participation of all of us—is to discover new ways of being together. Our old ways of relating to each other don't support us any longer, whether it's at home, in community, at work, or as nation states" (*Leadership and the New Science*, xi).

7. Charles Taylor describes the term *social imaginary* as "the way in which [people] imagine their social existence, how they fit together with others, how things go on between them and their fellows, the expectations which are normally met, and the deeper normative notions and images which underlie these expectations" (*Secular Age*, 171).

8. John 17:21.

The church has, too often, adopted the patterns of engagement that mirror those found in the larger culture rather than employing the art of relational Christlikeness to deal with difficult challenges. On important issues of life and faith, we tend to lean more toward anger, polarization, and fragmentation than we do toward reflection, listening, and unity. In some instances, we aren't content with just repositioning the furniture; we either nail it to the floor or set it on fire and throw it out into the street.

Leonard Sweet makes an important declaration about the way forward for the church:

> The way to save the world is not through more rules to live by, but through right relationships to live for. People are fast losing the art of being with one another. So it's not surprising that the number one problem in the world is people's living disconnected lives. They are detached from God, from others, and from creation. People are losing the art of living with one another.[9]

Save the world?[10] Such a declaration cannot even be considered unless followers of Jesus reflect deeply on the nature of their corporate identity—in other words, on what it really means to be *The Church*.

Such reflection does not begin with our creeds and confessions, or our doctrines and propositions. True to our great scriptural legacy, it all begins with a story.[11]

---

9. Sweet, *Out of the Question*, 1.

10. James Davison Hunter speaks of the church being the expression and demonstration of the kind of world that God is saving: "Until God brings forth the new heaven and the new earth, he calls believers, individuals and as a community, to conform to Christ and embody within every part of their lives, the shalom of God" (*To Change the World*, 230).

11. N. T. Wright sees the story of our Scriptures as a living narrative, one in which we participate in the present time: "We read scripture in order to be refreshed in our memory and understanding of the story within which we ourselves are actors, to be reminded where it has come from and where it is going to, and hence what our own part within ought to be" (*Last Word*, 115). Bartholomew and Goheen contrast the concept of the Bible as disconnected fragments with the Bible as a formative narrative: "Many of us have read the Bible as if it were merely a mosaic of little bits—theological bits, moral bits, historical-critical bit, sermon bits, devotional bits. But when we read the Bible in such a fragmented way, we ignore its divine author's intention to shape our lives through its story" (*Drama of Scripture*, 12).

A Biblical Overview

The ancient Hebrew people were miraculously rescued from their long-term slavery in Egypt. The way they looked at the world had been reformed over several generations by the influences and social structures of the Pharaoh's rule. Now, this mysterious God of the burning bush, this *I AM* who revealed himself to Moses, brought the people to a new corporate life. But who was this God? Was this God just one that was more powerful than the gods of Egypt? How would life under the God of the Hebrews differ from life under the ever-present glare of the Egyptian sun god, *Ra*?[12]

It was to these people—the people who still carried the experience of the Exodus within their memories—that these startling words were given:

> In the beginning, God created the heavens and the earth. The earth was without form and void, and darkness was over the face of the deep. And the Spirit of God was hovering over the face of the waters.
> And God said, "Let there be light," and there was light. (Gen 1:1–3)

A dramatic theological reorientation is taking place in these words. The people who had once been shackled by Pharaoh—the earthly personification of the Egyptian sun god—were being reformed by the God who had rescued them from Egypt. The vital theological implication of these opening words of Genesis are that the God the Hebrew people had come to know—the God of liberation—was not a territorial deity with greater power than other gods. This God was the only God, both creator and rescuer God, the God who put the sun in its proper place, ultimately demoting it to the fourth day of creation.[13]

Genesis chapters 1 and 2 tell the story of creation and describe a world that exists in the unhindered presence of God—a world that the ancient

---

12. "Most important of all the [Egyptian] gods was Re or Ra, the sun god. The pharaoh was his physical son and earthly embodiment" (*Baker Encyclopedia of the Bible*, 673). However, linking heavenly bodies with gods and goddesses was not limited to the Egyptians: "That [the creation] was all 'good' reflects God's wisdom and justice. At the same time the text shows subtle ways of disagreeing with the perspective of the ancient Near East. Most notable is the fact that it avoids using names for the sun and moon, which to the neighbors of the Israelites were also the names of the corresponding deities, and refers instead to the great light and the lesser light" (*IVP Bible Background Commentary*, 28–29).

13. "Exodus precedes Genesis in the same way that knowledge of God as Redeemer precedes knowledge of God as Creator" (Anderson, *Soul of Ministry*, 3).

Hebrews could only imagine. The narrative describes a created order that enjoys an integrative peace, and human beings find their identities in open relationship with one another and with the God who relished all that had been created.[14]

By the third chapter of Genesis, however, it all goes to ruin. The people turn away from God, and their relationships with him, with one another, and the whole of creation becomes damaged, seemingly without the possibility of repair. It is clear to see that there is a problem in the universe, both theologically and existentially. The ancient Hebrew people recognized that their life of slavery under Pharaoh was a particular distortion of the ideal of human existence, and now Genesis identifies the cosmic dimension of that distortion.

Chapters 4 through 11 then describe a series of potential solutions gone awry:

> *New children are born.* Maybe the next generation will clean things up. Instead, murder and deceit are birthed as a jealous offspring kills his own brother, lying to God about the desperate act.[15]

> *A global disaster cleans the slate.* God brings about a worldwide flood that destroys all life on earth, leaving only a righteous remnant that will start things anew. But as soon as dry land is found, the patriarch Noah becomes drunk and curses his own son, consigning him to a life of slavery under the rule of his brothers.[16]

> *Human ingenuity rises to the occasion.* As families, tribes and communities expand, common language and new developments in technology suggest the possibility that people can, by their own creativity, rise above the brokenness of the world. They build an iron-age monument to human power that is designed to reach up into God's presence, and God unravels it, lest the people overshoot their boundaries.[17]

---

14. Not only does God repeatedly call the creation "good" throughout Genesis 1, but he also enjoys the garden of paradise "at the time of the evening breeze" (Gen 3:8 NRSV).

15. Gen 4:1–16.

16. Gen 9:20–27.

17. Gen 11:1–9. John Goldingay points out that the name Babel suggests that the intention of the project was to give humans their own contrived access to God: "God's frustrating their attempt to build a tower with its top in the heavens prevents them from

Nothing works. Perhaps there is no solution to the universal problem that confronts all human societies: The world is not as it should be. People were intended for a shared life, characterized by peace rather than violence, plenty rather than poverty, life rather than death.

In Genesis chapter 12, however, the solution is provided. It is not an answer, however, that is grounded in human effort or ingenuity. The answer comes at the initiation of God:

> Now the Lord said to Abram, "Go from your country and your kindred and your father's house to the land that I will show you. I will make of you a great nation, and I will bless you, and make your name great, so that you will be a blessing. I will bless those who bless you, and the one who curses you I will curse; and in you all the families of the earth shall be blessed" (Gen 12:1–3 NRSV)

It is in these words that the core identity of God's people will be found. It is an identity that is forged through relationship with God, for the sake and blessing of the world.

When Jesus comes into the story, he understands that Israel has not fulfilled its Abrahamic destiny and is once again a captive people, shaped and formed by a roller coaster ride of generational corruption that ended with the collapse of a divided nation, exile, and domination under the boot heel of foreign oppressors. Jesus finds an Israel that has lost its moorings and only seems to know how to define itself in terms of its separation from the world. Jesus, however, has a broader agenda. The Gospel of Matthew offers these final words of Jesus, ones that echo the call from God to Abram:

> All authority in heaven and on earth has been given to me. Go therefore and make disciples of all nations, baptizing them in the name of the Father and of the Son and of the Holy Spirit, and teaching them to obey everything that I have commanded you. And remember, I am with you always, to the end of the age. (Matt 28:18b–20)

The ethnic furniture of the new, emerging church is moved around as Jesus shows that the church's essential nature comes at the initiation of God, and is characterized as a shared life of the people before God, not to

---

building a 'gate of God,' a means of gaining access to God's presence . . . That is not to say there is no possibility of movement between earth and heaven. It is to say that such movement lies in God's gift" (*Old Testament Theology*, 190).

the exclusion of the world, but for the sake of the world.[18] Lesslie Newbigin helps us with this:

> The Bible, then, is covered with God's purpose of blessing for all the nations. It is concerned with the completion of God's purpose in the creation of the world and of man within the world. It is not—to put it crudely—concerned with offering a way of escape for the redeemed soul out of history, but with the action of God to bring history to its true end. The Old Testament therefore is full of visions of a restored humanity living in peace and happiness within a renewed creation. These visions are not of an otherworldly bliss, but of earthly happiness and prosperity (Psalms 82 and 144), of wise and just government, of a renewed nature in which kindness has replaced the laws of the jungle (Isaiah 1:1–9).
>
> But this universal purpose of blessing is not to be effected by means of a universal revelation to all humanity. There is . . . a process of selection: a few are chosen to be the bearers of the purpose; they are chosen, not for themselves, but the sake of all.[19]

Newbigin frames the doctrine of election as part of God's work on behalf of the world. He shows that election is not a static, positional state of being, but rather a dynamic, relational work, intended for the blessing of the world. This election lies at the heart of what it means to be the church.

A Personal Ministry Transformation

> The Ascension does not mean that he is no longer the "sent one." We don't take over Jesus's ministry. It is still his ministry, which he continues in and through us. We carry it forward into paths where it has never gone before.
>
> —*Leonard Sweet*[20]

I planted a church in my mid-forties and truly hoped that it would be a church for the sake of the world. I believed that God would begin to work

---

18. Karl Barth saw the church's existence in the world as bound to the need of the world: "As God exists for [the world] in His divine way, and Jesus Christ in His divine-human, so the Christian community exists for it in its own purely human. All ecclesiology is grounded, critically limited, but also positively determined by Christology; and this applies in respect of the particular statement which here concerns us, namely, that the Church exists for the world" (*Church Dogmatics*, IV.3.2, 786).

19. *Open Secret*, 33–34.

20. *Out of the Question . . . Into the Mystery*, 198.

in people's lives once we instigated the process through evangelistic endeavors. I read the books on church planting and went to the seminars on church growth, and I was confident that if we related effectively to the culture around us, unchurched people would flock to our doors.

I was wrong.

Some fine people did join up, but they were mostly from other churches, or at least had come from church backgrounds. Over time, as I thought, prayed, and studied, I became convinced of something that challenged my former assumptions: While God's desires and intentions were for the whole world,[21] he wasn't waiting for us to arrive on the scene so that he could start touching the lives of people. Instead, I learned that God was already at work in that world before I showed up.[22]

There was a popular pub within walking distance of my office, and I decided to have lunch there every Tuesday. Over time, I learned the names of some of the regulars and the people who worked there. I ran into the bartender in a local coffee shop one morning, and we struck up a friendship. I discovered that he was a serious spiritual seeker, and, like most of the people I had come to know in the pub, had come from a very damaged relational background. He and I got together for breakfast on a regular basis to talk about life, faith, and anything else that came up.

My friendship with the bartender helped to create a sense of trust among the others in the pub. I invited my friend and two of the waitresses to have dinner at my home once a week to expand our conversations about the big questions of life. We shared those evenings together for three months, and they were among my most cherished experiences as a pastor.

I considered this pub to be part of my life of ministry—part of my parish, if you will. Through my relationships there I officiated at a wedding, performed a backyard baby dedication, and prayed for others. Every week when I would settle into my chair for lunch, someone in the pub would

---

21. See Gen 12:1–3; John 3:16; 2 Cor 5:11–21.

22. Eugene Peterson offers a helpful reflection on God's initiating work and reminds us of the term *prevenience*: "The cure of souls is a cultivated awareness that God has already seized the initiative. The traditional doctrine defining this truth is prevenience: God everywhere and always seizing the initiative . . . Prevenience is the conviction that God has been working diligently, redemptively, and strategically before I appeared on the scene" (*Contemplative Pastor*, 60). Lesslie Newbigin also values the concept: "I have spoken of mission in three ways. It is the proclamation of the kingdom, the presence of the kingdom, and the prevenience of the kingdom. By proclaiming the reign of God over all things the church acts out its faith that the Father of Jesus is indeed ruler of all" (*Open Secret*, 64).

wander over just to talk, giving tacit affirmation to the recognition that the pastor was *in*.

I had to let go of my expectations during this time. My bartender friend helped me see that I shouldn't consider people my projects, but instead I needed to be present to them, love them, and gently continue to bear witness to Jesus. I'd like to say that many of the people at this pub made public commitments to Christ, but I cannot. Even though a few of them visited my church, they found the experience to be unworkable. But they were insistent that I make my weekly showing on their turf. I continued to do that for seven or eight years.

I did, however, discover that God was truly at work. As I heard people's stories of life and tragedy, of addiction and abandonment, of hope and desperation, I began to suggest to them places in their lives where I saw God at work. I found them to be amazingly open to that possibility, and not put off by the idea of God at all. In fact, each person who talked with me acknowledged an awareness of some kind of spiritual presence that was helping them along their journey in life.[23] These were not people who weighed the relative merits of doctrinal specificities or who found meaning in right ecclesial affiliations. For them, what mattered was being in a relationship with someone who served as a willing spiritual director of sorts—someone who cared about them, loved them, and showed them more of the face of God than I had expected.

As I read the gospels, I see this kind of work in the ministry of Jesus as he rearranged the religious furniture of his contemporaries. Yes, he debated theology with the leaders who stood at the center of Israel's religious life, but his relationships with the marginalized people were different. He seemed to have a willingness to go to them and be present to them without demanding their adherence to particular religious standards, yet refusing to diminish who he was and what he was about.[24] It must be observed that his relational outreach drew harsh criticism, primarily from the local Jewish leaders, who claimed his miraculous works were blasphemous and demonically inspired, and that his care for the people on the margins of

---

23. Although each one could cite a reason why past church experiences would keep them from engaging with God through organizational means, whether Catholic, Protestant, or otherwise.

24. After Jesus' radical process of theological deconstruction and reconstruction in Matt 5–7, he engages in a series of transformational acts of healing in the lives of people marginalized by illness (8:1–4, 14–17; 9:1–8, 27–34), ethnicity (8:5–13), demonic oppression (8:28–34), and death (9:18–26).

religious respectability violated conventional holiness codes. It was his religious critics who labeled him "the friend of sinners."

Deep Trust in Jesus

> How a person lives speaks much more loudly than what he or she asserts, now as always. And with Christians nearly identical to all others in the culture, what they say loses its impact.
>
> —*Leonard Sweet*[25]

The early centuries of the Christian movement were marked by persecution, preaching, care for the poor, ministry to the sick, signs and wonders, and deep theological and intellectual development.[26] Christians, however, made up only about ten percent of the population of the Roman Empire by the beginning of the fourth century, when Constantine endorsed Christianity as the preferred religion of the empire.[27] During those pre-Constantine years, Christians had a significant impact on their world, but the impact was the result of their faithful presence rather than their cultural dominance.

As the church's place in contemporary Western culture is increasingly marginalized, pastors and other Christian leaders are still called to guide faithful people in the way of Jesus, and to do so in the context of the world. Some might claim that people in the church need biblical literacy and a deeper sense of theology, which is probably true. Others might insist that a stronger sense of community is needed, which is also probably true. Still others are attempting new and exciting expressions of church, which should be welcomed and encouraged. The managing of our ecclesiastical furnishings continues, with various and differing views of the hope for the ultimate arrangement.

These endeavors are, however, not ends in themselves, but rather signs that point to a deeper reality. Even our Scriptures themselves, according to Jesus, are not a stop sign but rather a flashing neon light that signals something better ahead. As he declared to his detractors:

---

25. *Out of the Question . . . Into the Mystery*, 21.

26. The 10-volume set *Ante-Nicene Fathers* (Peabody: Hendrickson, 1996) bears witness to this activity.

27. Rodney Stark projects a growth rate of 40 percent per decade, and estimates over six million Christians in the Roman Empire by the year 300 CE—approximately 10.5 percent of the overall population (*Rise of Christianity*, 4–13).

> You search the scriptures because you think that in them you have eternal life; and it is they that testify on my behalf. (John 5:39)

Truth is important to us, and we are often scandalized when a claim is made that truth is relative, situational, or irrelevant. Christians seek to be true to their faith, and it is a faith grounded in the One who claimed to be "the way, the truth, and the life."[28] While our understanding about what is true may be expressed in our doctrines, creeds, and ecclesiologies, truth runs deeper than all of those expressions. Leonard Sweet makes this distinction: "Truth is a lived relationship, not a set of rules for living or a list of views about the divine. Truth is not certainty, nor is it doubt—both of which reject Christ. Instead, it is mystery."[29]

This mystery, which is Jesus Christ, may not be fully comprehensible, but it is certainly, to some degree, knowable. If our understandings drive us toward unchallengeable certainty, however, then we run the risk of forgetting about God. When defined as having all the right, indisputable answers, certainty can set boundaries and close off the canons of thought and reflection, needing nothing more—perhaps, not even needing God. Confidence, however, is something else. Confidence demands trust, and trust is a relational concept.[30] Our confidence in the mystery that is Christ results in a relationship of trust that allows us to be drawn into his work in the world in order to engage our lives with the people he loves. As the apostle Paul affirms,

> Such is the confidence that we have through Christ toward God. Not that we are competent of ourselves to claim anything as coming from us; our competence is from God, who has made us competent to be ministers of a new covenant, not of letter but of spirit; for the letter kills, but the Spirit gives life. (2 Cor 3:3–6)

---

28. John 14:6.

29. Sweet, *Out of the Question*, 69.

30. Lesslie Newbigin affirms the need for knowledge to be grounded in our trust in God, and assigns at least partial responsibility to René Descartes for causing the isolation of human knowledge from God: "In spite of the role that the Supreme Being plays in Descartes's method, it did not take long for the critical principle to remove God from the realm of certain knowledge. Whatever his intentions, Descartes bequeathed to Europe a confidence that certain knowledge could be achieved without reference to God . . . But if the biblical story is true, the kind of certainty proper to a human being will be one which rests on the fidelity of God, not upon the competence of the human knower. It will be a kind of certainty which is inseparable from gratitude and trust" (*Proper Confidence*, 28).

There is an important task for Christian leadership in these challenging times. Rather than teaching people to hunker down and bolt the doors against the encroachment of culture, or to go to war with our brothers and sisters in Christ over theories of the atonement or the significance of baptism, perhaps the art of spiritual direction[31] can be embraced as a new way of being the church for the sake of the world. Along with our efforts toward social justice, care for the sick and poor, and other acts of kindness and compassion, we might also be taught to open our eyes and ears to what God is doing in the world and to discern what is an authentic work of the Spirit and what is merely another cultural or religious trend. As we learn about God's presence in worship and Christian community, we may also experience his presence in the faces of those who see themselves as outside God's circle of love.

As the furniture of our faith continues to be moved around, rebuilt and reupholstered, perhaps some new items can be moved into this household we call the church. Soft couches and chairs might provide rest for weary strangers and wanderers. New, expanded dining tables would have places for all who respond to the invitation of Jesus to come and dine, sharing together bread and wine, body and blood, finding seats crafted from the worthiness of Christ.

The ones who share a common life in this newly renovated house would arrive with eyes wide open and with ears alert to the Spirit, eager to see and hear what God the Father is doing in those who tremble at the call of Jesus to *come*. And the newly arranged furniture would provide a welcome rest for those responding to that invitation.

Bibliography

Anderson, Ray S. *The Shape of Practical Theology: Empowering Ministry with Theological Praxis*. Downers Grove: InterVarsity, 2001.

---

31. Eugene Peterson speaks of the relational dimension of spiritual direction: "Spiritual direction takes place when two people agree to give their full attention to what God is doing in one (or both) of their lives and seek to respond in faith" (*Working the Angles*, 150). Christiansen and Laird refer to Henri Nouwen's preference for "the term *spiritual friendship*, or *soul friend*, which conveyed the necessary give-and-take in the process of spiritual accountability and faith formation" (Nouwen, *Spiritual Direction*, ix). While practitioners of the art of spiritual direction would see it primarily as a process between two Christians, I would suggest that the skills of the spiritual director can be applied to Christian's relationships with people in the world beyond the church.

———. *The Soul of Ministry: Forming Leaders for God's People*. Louisville: Westminster John Knox, 1997.

Barth, Karl. *Church Dogmatics*. Vol. 4. Peabody: Hendrickson, 2010.

Bartholomew, Craig G., and Michael W. Goheen. *The Drama of Scripture: Finding Our Place in the Biblical Story*. Grand Rapids: Baker Academic, 2004.

Elwell, Walter A. *Baker Encyclopedia of the Bible*. Vol. 1. Grand Rapids: Baker, 1988.

Goldingay, John. *Old Testament Theology: Israel's Gospel*. Downers Grove: IVP Academic, 2003.

Hunter, James Davison. *To Change the World: The Irony, Tragedy, and Possibility of Christianity in the Late Modern Period*. New York: Oxford University Press, 2010.

Newbigin Lesslie. *The Open Secret: An Introduction to the Theology of Mission*. Grand Rapids: Eerdmans, 1995.

———. *Proper Confidence: Faith, Doubt & Certainty in Christian Discipleship*. Grand Rapids: Eerdmans, 1995.

Nouwen, Henri. *Spiritual Direction: Wisdom for the Long Walk of Faith*. New York: HarperOne, 2006.

Peterson, Eugene H. *The Contemplative Pastor: Returning to the Art of Spiritual Direction*. Grand Rapids: Eerdmans, 1989.

———. *Working the Angles: The Shape of Pastoral Integrity*. Grand Rapids: Eerdmans, 1987.

Rosen, Christine. "The Image Culture." *New Atlantis*, fall 2005. http://www.thenewatlantis.com/archive/10/rosen.htm.

Stark, Rodney. *The Rise of Christianity: How the Obscure, Marginal Jesus Movement Became the Dominant Religious Force in the Western World in a Few Centuries*. San Francisco: HarperCollins, 1997.

Sweet, Leonard. *Out of the Question . . . Into the Mystery: Getting Lost in the Godlife Relationship*. Colorado Springs: WaterBrook, 2004.

Taylor, Charles. *A Secular Age*. Cambridge: Harvard University Press, 2007.

Tickle, Phyllis. *Emergence Christianity: What It Is, Where It Is Going, and Why It Matters*. Grand Rapids: Baker, 2012.

Walton, John H., et al. *The IVP Bible Background Commentary: Old Testament*. Downers Grove: InterVarsity, 2000.

Wheatley, Margaret J. *Leadership and the New Science: Discovering Order in a Chaotic World*. San Francisco: Berrett-Koehler, 1999.

Wright, N. T. *The Last Word: Beyond the Bible Wars to a New Understanding of the Authority of Scripture*. San Francisco: HarperSanFrancisco, 2005.

11

EPIC Parenting in the Post-Church Church

Rich Melheim, DMin

Part 1: Préjà Vu

THERE IS NO REASON to be a student of the future unless, of course, you plan to spend the bulk of the rest of your life there.

Some people experience déjà vu. They momentarily relive something they feel happened before. When it comes to the church, I think stewards of the future would do well to train themselves in the practice of a little préjà vu. Take a look at the trends and attitudes young adults have toward religion, church and church attendance, and you'll see something that hasn't happened yet—but is going to happen soon.

When my dad taught me how to drive, he told me one thing that stuck in my mind: *Don't look at the taillights of the car in front of you. Look at the taillights of the car in front of the car in front of you. Whatever that car does, the car in front of you is sure to follow.*

Travel with me a moment into the world of the car in front of the car in front of the church—the next batch of young parents. Consider for a moment how they view the church and their role in it. Then, let's explore an EPIC[1] (Experiential, Participatory, Image-Driven, Connective) formula

---

1. Sweet, *Postmodern Pilgrims*, xxi.

Christian leaders might embrace in order to grow faith at its most elemental level in breadth and depth in the post-church church.

First, a pulse check.

The Sinking of the Member Ship

> If the people don't want to come to the ballpark how are you going to stop them?
>
> —*Yogi Berra*

The bulk of young people today are not interested in church membership. Most have already formed their meaningful communities. Most are not interested in what we consider standard corporate worship. It doesn't resonate with them enough for them to make any room for one more commitment on their overly packed schedules. They aren't interested in what we call fellowship. They already have too many friends, circles, and clubs demanding their attention. Sunday is their only day off, and that day is jam packed from predawn to dusk with sports and friends and activities.

Pew on the Empty Pew

A recent study commissioned by the Pew Forum on Religion & Public Life offers sobering statistics regarding the next generation of parents and the future of the church:

> By some key measures, Americans ages 18 to 29 are considerably less religious than older Americans. Fewer young adults belong to any particular faith than older people do today. They also are less likely to be affiliated than their parents' and grandparents' generations were when they were young. Fully one-in-four members of the Millennial generation—so called because they were born after 1980 and began to come of age around the year 2000—are affiliated with any particular faith. Indeed, Millennials are significantly more unaffiliated than members of Generation X were at a comparable point in their life cycle (20% in the late 1990s) and twice as unaffiliated as Baby Boomers were as young adults (13% in the late 1970s). Young adults also attend religious services less often than older Americans today. And compared with their elders

today, fewer young people say that religion is very important in their lives.[2]

It's not that young adults don't believe in God. A mere 5 percent admit to being atheists.[3] This demographic has faith. They just don't see religion and church as necessary parts of their faith fabric.

The bigger problem is this: it is not merely those who have lost faith who are leaving the church and not coming back. In the past ten years, approximately fifty million Christians left the church.[4] The percentage attending worship has eroded from half of all Americans to less than a third.[5] By the end of the next decade, surveys indicate 40 percent of all church-attending Christians will be worshipping God, serving others, and studying the Bible outside of the congregational setting.[6] Among twenty-somethings, 60 percent say they do not see church as the best place to pursue their faith.[7]

The Young and the Churchless

> There are basically three kinds of people. Those who let things happen. Those who make things happen. And those who don't know anything happened.
>
> —*Sir Winston Churchill*

Here's the good news: In a major survey of thirteen to seventeen year olds in America, 75 percent actually call themselves Christian.[8] Two out of three teens say they pray to God every day.[9] There is a huge interest in general spirituality, in care for the environment, in social justice, and in putting faith into action by getting hands dirty on mission projects. Yet, a significant shift is taking place among this group that demands a wakeup call for anyone with half a heart—and half a brain—for the future of the church.

A recent survey released by the Barna Group showed technology and social networking reconfiguring teens' expressed needs for

2. Pew, "Religion among the Millennials."
3. Ibid.
4. "Love Jesus, Hate Church Index," December 1, 2010.
5. Ibid.
6. Ibid.
7. Miller, *iKids*, 164.
8. Dean, *Almost Christian*, 201.
9. Barna, *Real Teens*, 26.

spiritual engagement at church.[10] Although attendance at youth group events is slightly up for mainline Protestant kids, once the high school fun is done, the following are all on the decline:

- Prayer
- Bible reading
- Giving money to and through the church
- Sunday school attendance
- Worship attendance

Even among the most zealous "born again" teens, the number who said they "shared their faith with another person in the last year" dropped from two-thirds in 1997 to less than half in 2009. And once high school youth group is over and the diploma is in hand, church becomes just "one more thing" to do on an already too-busy schedule. Worship is seen as a poor use of time. Faith practices in the home have become rare options. Identity and community have been formed elsewhere, and although they are more than fine with the concept of church, it no longer merits their attention nor meets their needs.

All this makes a steward of the future church wonder: Is this attitude a symptom of a larger dis-ease within the church, or is it the disease, itself? Kenda Creasy Dean, associate professor of youth, church and culture at Princeton Theological Seminary and author on youth trends, writes:

> While religion is seldom a source of conflict for teenagers (the good news), it is also seldom a source of identity (the bad news) . . . While sociologists have long demonstrated known religious beliefs and practices do, in fact, shape the values and lifestyles of U.S. adolescents, teens themselves tend to think of religion as wall paper: it's an accepted part of their lives that stays in the background, and therefore doesn't merit much thought.[11]

Doesn't merit much thought? How did we, the church, miss that target? If it doesn't merit much thought, it evidently didn't have much meaning.

---

10. Ibid.
11. Dean, *Almost Christian*, 164.

The Real Hunger Games

Young people today are not looking for history. They are searching for mystery. They are not hungry for memberships. They are starving for meaning. They are not longing for programs. They're longing for belonging. And instead of the steaming, savory multigrain fresh bread of life and the intoxicating hot wine/blood of a radical (of the root) Jesus, they see the church as offering them a bland, tasteless Styrofoam lily-white wafer and the cheapest excuse for a sickeningly sweet Costco wine we can find.

And they sip, and they slip, and they ship away into the shadows to find their true meaning, true identity, true community, true faith connection among a small groups of personal friends, a wider but select circle of online confidants, and a world of choices and voices totally apart from the cold stone walls of the church that tried its best to warmly love, nurture, teach and reach them in one hour a week with its well-meaning professional staff and its pile of well-warmed programs.

Coming Back

Thirty-three years of ministry with children, youth and families, twenty years of traveling the world in search of healthy family faith incubation systems, and three years with Len Sweet at George Fox on a doctoral journey have brought me to a stark contusion (*sic*): It's not that the children won't come back. They can't come back.

You can't come back to a place you've never been.

Their bodies may have been in church. Their seats may have been in the pews. Their names may have been recorded on a Sunday school roster. They may have sat for a decade-plus dutifully doodling on a children's bulletin, eating Cheerios from a Ziploc bag and pretending to listen while the band played on. Their bodies were there, but for an increasing number of our teens and young adults, their hearts and minds were off in a galaxy far, far away. Their parents dropped them off at a church choked full of programs and went out for coffee, thus showing them that church was for children. The education methods they endured and connect-the-dots children's bulletins they were handed proved less than engaging. Most of the time they sat as simple spectators in someone else's show. "Sit still while I instill" was the unspoken message. The youth's gifts and talents were rarely challenged, held up or celebrated in the body. Their questions were rarely drawn out and wrestled with honestly, openly by fellow seekers and strugglers. Worship was rarely what Len Sweet calls EPIC. Preaching was occasionally relevant but their preachers—who were taught to preach by professors who were taught to preach long before the internet era—had little clue how to use current technology. In a post-Gutenberg world of right-brain images, music and pictures, the left-brain sermons were a mile over their heads and light years away from their hearts. Old World preaching was cold-word preaching. It often left them numb and bored and disengaged.

The Parental Vacuum

At church our youth were rarely exposed to the wisdom of the elders. At home, they never talked faith with their parents. As little children in a Christian home, they may have even gone to bed hearing the stories of faith, saying their prayers and singing the songs of faith with Mommy or Daddy by their bedside. But as they grew too old for that, they closed their doors and closed their minds and closed their parents out. At both church and school, they grew up segregated mostly from their parents. They spent most of their time with peers. They found their counsel, companionship, identity and meaning most powerfully and profoundly in the presence of a handful of flesh-and-blood friends. This was a family of a different sort—peers who texted them a hundred times a day. Friends who knew more about them than their own parents did. All this identity, all this meaning happened— and is happening—virtually and completely apart from the church. Their bodies may have been in church all those years, but their hearts and minds were not. They were there, but they were never really there when they were there. All of this is telling me that they won't be back. They can't be back.

Again, you can't come back to a place you've never been.

Kendra Creasy Dean writes:

> We are doing an exceedingly good job of teaching youth what we really believe: namely, that Christianity is not a big deal, that God requires little, and that the church is a helpful social institution filled with nice people focused primarily on "folks like us"—which, of course, begs the question of whether we are really the church at all. Teenagers tend to approach religious participation, like music and sports, as an extracurricular activity: a good, well-rounded

thing to do, but unnecessary for an integrated life. What we have been less able to convey to young people is faith.[12]

We haven't conveyed faith? Whoa! Isn't that at least a part of why we were here? Why we put all the energy and effort into children, youth and family programs over the last fifty years? Why we built the education wing, hired the youth staff, set up all the slick programs?

The Meaning of Faith and the Faith of Meaning

What the Christian faith is not to this waiting, wandering, blundering, pondering, wondering, plundering, needing, bleeding, full-housed-empty-homed, full-scheduled-empty-lifed generation is exactly what it is: a faith of meaning. Ultimate meaning. Close-your-eyes-in-death-with-a-twinkle-in-your-eyes-and-a-grave-shattering-shout-of-victory-on-your-lips meaning.

What Jesus is not to this beautifully talented and passionate generation of livers and lovers, is exactly who he is: someone they unknowingly hunger for, cry for, bleed for and just might die for. Real meaning. Real love.

A real reason to dream, to act, to hope, to attack the countless impossible windmills their young lives will encounter.

A timeless face and a real-time place and a song and a race that rages against the Pharisees, and ultimately dares them to ultimately matter as if they actually, factually infect, influence, inform and transform their world for good. And forever.

As a lover of both Christ and his bride, all I can say to this dangerous day is this:

My God, my God—and I say this with a literal tear in my eye—*why have we forsaken you? What has this church done? We have turned your tougher-than-nails Son into a soft and sweet ineffectual storybook character. We have turned your broken body into tasteless Styrofoam wafers and your priceless blood into the weakest of worthless wine.*

My God, my God—and I say this with a literal tear in my heart—*how have we forsaken you? In our hands and on our watch we have let the Word made Flesh become the flesh made words. Empty words. Boring words. Too many words spoken with too little meaning, read from a book with no more energy than the waiter reading the menu at Subway.*

---

12. Ibid., 202.

And we wonder why the kids don't come back? The bride of Christ has lost both interest in and passion for her husband. And the children don't want to come home to such a sad and sorry empty house. They won't. They can't.

We saw to it. They saw through it. And it's time to undo it.

Now.

Part II: EPIC Parenting in the Post-Church Church

The best way to predict the future is to invent it.

—Alan Kay

I once tweeted my friend Len Sweet with the quote: "The home altar will alter the home." Within minutes, he texted back: "The altar ego will alter the id."

In this Festschrift, Brit Jason Clark writes: "God's people in exile, his people living amongst a world of people who don't know God, are invited to live in a particular way."

There is one relatively easy way to solve the problem of young parents not bringing themselves and their children to church: Bring the church to their homes. Name and claim and reframe the home as a little church. Then equip it to be the church "when they lie down and when they rise."[13]

Let me suggest a particularly EPIC way that the post-church church might live and bring families to Christ as it brings Christ to families. I will suggest we implement this formula every night in every home. The formula is:

MDP + MEM + M3 = EPIC Parenting

FAITH5 x 7

Most dedicated people + most effective means +
most meaning-filled moments

Share + Read + Talk + Pray + Bless "every night in every home"
= EPIC Parenting

---

13. Deut 6:7 NRSV.

MDP—Enlist the Most Dedicated People

In order to midwife a miracle for the kids around the world, we've first got to midwife a miracle for the world around the kids.

This new formula will involve less of a program approach to Christian education at church and more of a process approach at home. As systems thinkers we cannot ignore the most important piece of a system and expect to fix anything. Parents have been, are, and always will be the most important piece of the faith incubation system. Parents we can't ignore. We need them at the core.

We will call on those who have the greatest access to children and the most at stake—parents—as primary faith teachers, mentors, guides and role models to their own children. We will challenge them to "do and be" what they once promised God they would do be when they first held their babies in their arms. The home will be reclaimed, renamed and reframed as the primary incubator of faith. Parents will be commissioned and called as pastors, shepherds and bishops to a little church to tend the little flock that is in their charge.

MEM—Engage the Most Effective Means

At the core of this systems change, a simple set of nightly faith practices will engage parents and children in being the church. The FAITH5 (Faith Acts in the Home) include:

1. *Share* the highs and lows of the day
2. *Read* a key scripture or story from Sunday's preaching or teaching text
3. *Talk* about how the highs and lows might relate to the verse
4. *Pray* for one another's highs and lows
5. *Bless* one another before turning off the lights on the day

Part of my doctoral research included teaching these themes from Australia to Korea to India to North America, and conducting six-week tests in sixty-five households from Columbia, Maryland, to Baton Rogue, Louisiana, to Sammamish Hills, Washington. Results and video stories of these "enrichuals" (faith practices) can be viewed at www.faith5.org.

MMM—Encounter at the Most Meaning-Full Moments

The epilogue in the book *Holding Your Family Together*[14] outlines the psychology, sociology and neurology of why "nighttime is the right time" to do your primary faith formation. It may be that nighttime is also the right time to bring the church home and inject the DNA of worship into the nucleus of the family cell. When you look carefully at the neurology of sleep and the ability parents and other caregivers have to plant thoughts of peace, love, understanding and care in the brain before drifting off to sleep, it becomes clear that the bedtime routine is the optimal time to impact the faith life of both children and adults. Nighttime is the right time to process the day, bond the family, seed dreams and set the stage for the Holy Spirit to whisper to the heart all night long. It may also be the most effective time to build and nurture the little post-church church. Let me pull some research from the *Holding Your Family Together* book:

Maximum Problem-Solving Mode

Current research on the nature of sleep suggests the optimal time for the brain to work on difficult problems is not during the working day, the classroom day, or even the waking hours. It turns out the best time to work on complex personal challenges, engage in deep reflection and discover creative solutions is actually . . . during sleep!

Contrary to common misassumptions, the brain doesn't go dormant when you doze off. Instead, it kicks into high meaning-making gear, processing the mountains of data collected throughout the day on your short-term "scratch pad" (hippocampus), connecting it to the myriad of existing information, memories and patterns already stored on your long term "hard drive" (neocortex), and flashing it all through the firings and wirings of your one hundred billion neurons in a rapid, churning, constant, relentless effort to make some sense of it all. The answers to life's most vexing problems are not best incubated, nurtured, taught and caught while making a macaroni Moses in Sunday school or sitting in a pew listening to the preacher's sermon. The most innovative answers to life's most complex challenges arise when your eyes are closed and you are deep and soundly asleep! Allow me to explain.

14. Ibid.

Searching the File Cabinets

According to molecular biologist Dr. John Medina, in the bestseller *Brain Rules*, the brain is not asleep when you are asleep. It is not resting at all. Rather, the brain kicks into maximum creative meaning-making mode. Medina believes the reason we need sleep is not to turn the brain off, but to turn the brain's learning power on. It appears that the sleeping brain shuts off outward stimuli in favor of inward stimuli and begins a concentrated hunt through the "file cabinets" of what you already know and have in storage, searching for connections, associations, and creative answers to any new challenges the day threw your way.

A Thousand Reruns

During REM sleep, much of what was important that day—and much of what was important enough to register but remain unnoticed—re-fires and rewires over and over thousands of times in the brain's attempt to make sense of it. Then, during slow-wave non-REM sleep, the brain takes those most memorable outward bits of new information—those things that connected with something that was already meaningful to you—and it sifts through the labyrinth of stored memories searching for associated connections, combinations of potential solutions and meaning. It takes the "new" and connects it to the "knew" in order to be helpful for the "you."

Dr. Sara Mednick, assistant professor of psychiatry at UC Diego, writes:

> For creative problems you've already been working on, the passage of time is enough to find solutions. However, for new problems, only REM sleep enhances creativity. REM sleep helps achieve such solutions by stimulating associative networks (i.e., looking around for connections to what you already know), and by allowing the brain to make new and useful associations between unrelated ideas.[15]

In other words, your conscious mind is great for working on old problems, but for new solutions to new problems, the subconscious mind is better equipped to go searching through unrelated file cabinets. With senses shut down and the gatekeepers and logic centers of the brain on break, your subconscious mind is free to seek out and find new and creative solutions to problems the conscious mind wouldn't even consider.

15. Sara Mednik, quoted in Kain, "Let Me Sleep On It."

The Psychology of Nighttime Rituals

Psychologically, having consistent, predictable bedtime rituals in place is healthy and comforting for a child. It gives children a sense of stability, predictability and control. Experiencing the consistency of a caring nightly ritual along with the thought "someone knows what I'm going through" right before bedtime helps to resolve issues and set the stage for better sleep. Children—and adults—who don't get enough sleep tend to focus on and remember the negative more than the positive. Lack of proper sleep leaves one irritable, jumpy and tense. Boys who continue with sleep disorders into adulthood have twice the risk of clinical depression. Girls with sleep problems experience depression at five times the normal rate.

Treating sleep disorders early and setting healthy patterns in place before the upheaval of puberty can dramatically improve psychiatric symptoms in adults. Ending the day with the caring conversation, prayer and blessing—as opposed to sharing it at meal time and spending the next few hours with television, texting and homework—allows the last messages your brain receives prior to drifting off to be positive messages. Here is where the psychology of nighttime blessing blurs into the neurology: Sharing, caring, massaging, laughing, singing and blessing all allow the brain to sop up cortisol from the bloodstream. This allows melatonin—the sleep drug—to do its duty. Cortisol, the stress hormone, kills baby nerve cells as they are born and instructs the body to hold on to all the fat it can. (Blessing as a brain-enhancer and weight loss technique)?

According to USC's Dr. David Agus, side effects of poor sleep are hypertension, confusion, memory loss, the inability to learn new things, obesity, cardiovascular disease, and depression.[16]

The Sociology of Nighttime Rituals

Sociologically, rituals are important for expressing, fixing and reinforcing shared values and beliefs. We are drawn to trust and appreciate anyone who shares in the ritual and gives us the gifts of time and attention. Returning to, reflecting upon and restating the challenges of the day aloud within the context of a safe, loving family or family of friends bonds us to those people. It turns the "me" into the "we" and the house into a home.

---

16. Agus, *End of Illness*, 240.

The Neurology of Nighttime Rituals

The strongest argument for FAITH 5™ at bedtime—as opposed to dinner or drive time—has to do with how the last few minutes of each day can set the stage for a night filled with neural networking, researching, creative problem-solving and solutions. With recent advances in technology allowing us to watch sleeping brains "real time", scientists have been able to determine that the areas of the brain controlling logic, expectations, and socially acceptable restraints are shut down during sleep. Areas associated with visual images, emotion, and perception of movement kick into high gear during sleep. With our senses, censors and logical areas turned off and the visual and emotional areas of the brain turned on, anything goes! Any wall can be flown over. Any dragon can be slain. Any problem can be solved. Computers are great for storing and analyzing vast quantities of information, but one thing artificial memory can't do well is to ruminate.

The human brain's brilliance comes from its ability to allow seemingly random, unrelated ideas and knowledge to collide with other random, unrelated ideas and thoughts. The collision of seemingly unrelated ideas is where most creativity and innovation springs forth: "You got your chocolate on my peanut butter!" or "You got your Bible verse on my low!" It is in this caldron of the adjacent possible where brilliant dreams are born. Sleep is the not merely the bedchamber of transient dreams. It is the neural crucible of creative innovation.

The Theology of Nighttime Rituals

"God speaks in one way, and in two, though people do not perceive it. In a dream, in a vision of the night, when deep sleep falls on mortals, while they slumber on their beds, then he opens their ears" (Job 33:14–16).

If you believe God can speak during waking hours, is it not possible God can speak during sleep? The Bible says, "Yes!" God does speak and reveal in dreams. We just need to have our ears on.

History is filled with insights and inventions released in dreams. Mendeleyev laid out the final form of the periodic table in a dream. Kekulé discovered the arrangement of the benzene molecule asleep. Mary Shelley literally dreamed up Frankenstein and Robert Lewis Stevenson received Dr. Jekyll and Mr. Hyde while asleep. Architect Solange Fabião designed the Museum of Ocean and Surf in a dream. Gandhi's call for a nonviolent movement to force the British from India came as a dream. Beethoven, Billy Joel and many other musicians received songs in their sleep. Then there's Jacob's ladder, Joseph's celestial dreams, the other Joseph's warning to flee to Egypt, and Peter's blanket full of unclean animals.

If sleep is the time best suited for creative problem-solving in God's beautifully designed brain, and if one-third of our lives are spent asleep, would it not be dreadfully poor stewardship of God *not* to speak to us in our dreams? And would it not be dreadfully poor stewardship for God's appointed guardians—parents—*not* to train their children to be ready to hear the still, small voice of God calling them in the night, and to prepare them nightly to answer?

In Conclusion

When you look at the car in front of the car—the children today who will one day be the parents themselves—it is clear that membership in a church structure that operates the way most churches operate today will not be their thing. Church attendance may not be on their radar. The current generation of young parents may be "in the church but not of it." The next generation of young Christian parents might just be "of the church, but not in it."

If that is even remotely the case, how might we best equip, train, motivate and call them to "be" the church at home? I'd say the training needs to start today with more of an experiential, participatory, image-driven and conversational worship/education blend at church that spills the scripture stories and community conversations over every night in every home.

This EPIC parenting formula is no silver bullet. It is not the "end all" and "be all" for the post-church church. But it is an experience—not a class. Do it right and you'll be known as the church with no class!

It is by its very nature participatory—not a show. EPIC parenting is no spectator's sport. By sharing highs and lows and bouncing them up against God's story, it is intimately and relevantly image-driven: engaging the text in the context of the most important images of the day. And by sharing, reading, talking, praying and blessing (FAITH5), it connects in deep community every night at the optimal moments to effect the brain in powerful, positive, long-term ways.

Enlisting the most dedicated people, engaging the most effective means at the most meaningful moments and encouraging each other in these EPIC ways are a liturgy for the post-church church:

The home.

Yes, the home altar will alter the home. And yes, Len, you are correct: The altar ego will alter the id.

Bibliography

Agus, David B. *The End of Illness*. New York: Free Press, 2011.
Barna, George. *Real Teens*. Ventura, CA: Gospel Light, 2001.
Berra, Yogi. *The Yogi Book*. Minneapolis: Workman, 1997.
Dean, Kenda Creasy. *Almost Christian: What the Faith of Our Teenagers Is Telling the American Church*. New York: Oxford University Press, 2010.
Kain, Debra. "Let Me Sleep On It: Creative Problem Solving Enhanced by REM Sleep." UC San Diego New Center, June 9, 2009. http://ucsdnews.ucsd.edu/archive/newsrel/health/06-09Mednick.asp.
"Love Jesus, Hate Church Index." *Lovejesushatechurch.com*. http://www.lovejesushatechurch.com/index.htm. Website no longer available.
McCranie, Steve. *Love Jesus, Hate Church: How to Survive in Church—or Die Trying*. [Gastonia, NC]: Back2Acts, 2005.
Miller, Craig Kennet. *iKids: Parenting in the Digital Age*. Nashville: Discipleship Resources, 2014.
Pew. "Religion among the Millennials." *Pewforum.org*. February 17, 2010. http://www.pewforum.org/2010/02/17/religion-among-the-millennials/#attendance.
Sweet, Leonard. *Postmodern Pilgrims*. Nashville: Broadman & Holman, 2000.

12

Discovering the Future, Hidden Deep within the Past

Brian A. Ross, DMin

>Postmodernity is more pre-modern than modern.
>
>—*Leonard Sweet*[1]

>As a historian of Christianity, I want the Church to lean back—not just back to the '50s, but all the way back through 2000 years of history . . . But at the same time, and I do mean simultaneously, we must use that energy and power that comes from "learning to lean" to kick forward into the future.
>
>—*Leonard Sweet*[2]

READING A BOOK BY Leonard Sweet, or simply asking him a question, can be similar to walking into a room where its occupants are exchanging knowing glances and whispering to one another. Immediately you have a sense that something important is being shared, but it may be quite some time until you understand what all the fuss is about.

The two quotations above are familiar to all of Len's students and quite possibly, to most of his readers. The first time I heard these words in a

---

1. Leonard Sweet, in discussion with the author, March 2013. See also Sweet et al., *A Is for Abductive*, 125.

2. Leonard Sweet, quoted in Burke, *Making Sense of Church*, 28–29.

discussion I registered that something of real significance had been offered. And of course, cognitively, I understood the big idea. But as any ministry leader has experienced, *comprehension* and *personal knowledge* are not quite the same thing. Registering solemn expressions, and noticing an individual whisper to another, is not the same thing as being let in on the secret.

A Personal Journey

For me, coming to faith in Jesus was much like finding an anchor. As a child of divorce and limited means, it seemed to me that I was influenced as much by Jack Tripper and Jim Morrison as I was by anyone else. I tried my best to fit into the milieu of the 1980s and early 1990s. Like my contemporaries, I dreamed about women, money, and athletic success. However, like our personal finances, I often came up short. But the absence of something does not exclude it from imprinting your soul. When I found Jesus, I found something that could tether my passions and unfulfilled longings.

Like the stereotype of a religious fundamentalist, faith in the Bible seemed to offer certainty and extreme moral clarity within the raging angsty seas of my generation. For the first time, I knew the Truth. For the first time, I knew what was Right and Wrong. For the first time, I knew I was on the Winning Side of everything.

But if you are securely anchored, you are not going anywhere.

Years of fundamentalist faith eventually took their toll. You cannot be cock sure with everyone and expect to be liked. You cannot continually wash the outside of the cup and assume the inside will automatically become spotless. You cannot close your eyes to the reality of the outside world and avoid running into an immovable object.

Several years later, fundamentalism simply was not working.

More than once I had needlessly offended human beings I was called to shepherd. More than once I found myself embarrassed by national Christian leaders I claimed to follow. More than once I looked at myself in the mirror and I knew the easy answers were in reality, no answers at all. So like many of my ministry colleagues in our twenties, I set out to become a new kind of pastor.

I learned that I could win points with people by complaining about the church.

I ascertained that I was invited to parties more often if I enjoyed all forms of progressive politics as much as the next guy.

I sized up that highlighting justice over inequality had more cache than calls of repentance.

I understood that sharing my personal struggles in great detail, led others to describe me as different, authentic, and real.

I noticed that quoting Joel Coen, rather than Jesus Christ, made it easier to make friends.

But once again, I was being tossed to and fro by the rising and crashing of the waves of the sea.

> Whoever marries the spirit of the age will find himself a widower in the next.
>
> —*William Ralph Inge*[3]

Coming to my senses, I tried again briefly to let down the anchor of conservative Evangelicalism. I believed I had simply left my first love. Once again, I needed to stand on the fundamentals of faith. But a man, no matter how sincere, cannot relive his youth. Yes, it was comforting to find some stability in the churning waters of early twenty-first-century life. But this time, there was no joy. I felt like I was prematurely aging. I was becoming a thirty-something prude. I was slowly once more becoming the prophetic pastor who only knew how to preach, "Thou Shalt Not!"

This was not going to work.

So I turned to C. S. Lewis.

Admittedly, some of his metaphors that dripped with fresh illumination in the mid-twentieth century no longer popped. But there was something different with his writings. They smelled of deeply spirit-filled, and yet all-too-human, Truth. Christ was the center, and yet he was not crassly clear and comprehensible. I moved on from the books Lewis wrote to books others wrote about him. I sized up that he was deeply Christian, and yet not quite Evangelical, nor a disciple of modernism. In fact, Lewis was downright medieval. (After all, he was a scholar of premodern literature.) And the Christianity of centuries ago, was something quite different from the Christianity I had been discipled and schooled within.

Lewis led to the wise and witty G. K. Chesterton. Chesterton led to the imaginative and visionary George MacDonald. MacDonald (somehow) led to the penetrating and startling Alasdair MacIntyre. MacIntyre led to the difficult and yet brilliant John Milbank. Milbank led to the clear and

---

3. Staub, *Culturally Savvy Christian*, 3.

comprehensive Charles Taylor. Taylor led to the unknown and unheralded Ivan Illich. And Illich led me back to my mentor and friend Leonard Sweet.

Sweet's right. The way to the future runs right through the past. Finding what's next begins with rediscovering what's been left behind.

I no longer needed an anchor. I discovered the rudder of what's gone before.

> Tradition means giving votes to the most obscure of all classes, our ancestors. It is the democracy of the dead. Tradition refuses to submit to the small and arrogant oligarchy of those who merely happen to be walking about.
>
> —G. K. Chesterton[4]

Leaning Back vs. Standing Straight

I quickly confess that I am not a historian or a theologian. What follows is primarily a personal vision of a bygone era that fuels my ministry in our hyper-modern world. It is much more the product of one's man imagination than that of academic research. And yet, I do believe there is something here for those who serve God's people.

What I *know* is that the best and brightest of the Christian community in say AD 1200, or 800, or 400, were not just like you and I. Not only did they live in different historical situations with different experiences, they quite literally lived out their faith in ways that were quite different from our late-modern world.

In what follows, I will tempt to summarize and contrast "premodern faith" (the Christian vision from the early church into the Middle Ages), "contemporary Christianity" (common tenets of today's conservative, American Evangelicalism), and "secular faith" (the assumptions of contemporary people who see little need for Christianity.) I hope that this will demonstrate that historic Christian orthodoxy is not quite the same thing that many of us modern people presuppose.

---

4. Chesterton, *Orthodoxy*, 45.

A Premodern Faith

When *I* read about the faith of Christians from long, long ago, the faith of those who ministered and prayed and dreamed before the Enlightenment, even before the printing press, these phrases and descriptions rise up into *my* vision:

God as Bigger and Nearer than I Can Fathom. God is the ever-present, uniting energy and power of all living beings and material objects. And yet, God is pure love, gift-giver, peace-maker and personably knowable.

Theological Truth as Received Wisdom. Theology is the learnable craft of the essential discoveries of Spirit-filled men and women through the ages. They were not infallible, but only a fool would try to reinvent the cumulative findings of millennia.

The Bible as Essential Narratives and Metaphors. Scripture contains the seminal stories and images of human and divine realities. They cannot be improved upon. Their invitation is to imaginatively combine our story with The Story.

Spirituality as Paying Attention. Knowing God is listening and watching for his unexpected work within the world and within us. It is less doing, and more seeing and hearing and responding accordingly.

Faith as Big Enough to Rest. Personal knowledge of God's presence leads to the ability to abandon manipulation. Nothing needs to be proven or won over and against others. He is Big and so we can sleep at night.

The Arts as Signs of God. Human creativity, in any form, is a reflection of God's image within us. Bringing order and beauty out of raw materials is a manifestation of God likeness.

Beauty of the Everyday. Every ordinary thing screams of extraordinary realities that lay beyond. The simple is a portal to the Ultimate.

Human Beings as Icons of the Divine. God is too big, too infinite, to be seen by mortals. Yet every man and woman, boy and girl, channels something about his unfathomable wonder.

Church as a Community of Remembering and Pointing. Gatherings of believers were never intended to be pleasing cloisters of the perfectly pious. Church is the theatre of remembering there is more going on than meets the eye and it is the sign post reminding us of Who to look towards.

Mission as a Nudge to Awaken and Dream. The vocation of faithful Christians is the call to tactfully and wisely tap others on the shoulder to the possibilities of incomprehensible love and beauty from the One who made them.

Judgment as Inevitably Chosen Trajectories. Final judgment of eternal life or deep death is truly the result of people finding what they were looking for. Whatever road we have chosen to travel simply continues even further on to the other side.

Contemporary Christianity

Without a doubt, contemporary Western Christianity contains echoes of an earlier manifestation. And certainly, there are numerous things within our times that are laudable and commendable. Yet I fear something has been lost. Mass production, capitalistic consumerism, and liberal democracy have molded a different kind of Christianity. Standing straight can create spiritual fatigue.

When *I* read and experience contemporary Christianity, these phrases and descriptions rise up into *my* vision:

God as an All Powerful, and Yet Distant Being. God is real. He is the maker of all that is seen and unseen, living in perfect holiness. He watches us from heaven, willing us to do the right thing.

Theological Truth as Quoting More Scripture. Theology is the logical and orderly science of comparing verses and words of the biblical text with other words and verses of the biblical text.

The Bible as Encyclopedia and Laws. The Bible is an indispensable source of true information and lists of acceptable ethical actions.

Spirituality as Rigorous Discipline. Personal devotion is learning to routinely engage spiritual practices regardless of one's feelings or desires. The more self-control one displays, the more they gain God.

Faith as Taking a Stand. Trust in God is most clearly displayed in running contrary with word and deed to the ways of the unbelieving world. A vocal minority is a faithful remnant.

The Arts as Dangerous Temptations. Human creativity is a gift from God. Yet, most cultural artifacts are hindrances and weights to true life and thus, are best to be avoided.

The Emptiness of the Everyday. Common life is simply that: common. It has been created by God; yet true Christian devotion will find a way to transcend its slumbering ways.

Human Beings as Potential Threats and Converts. Men and women, boys and girls, are either believers or unbelievers. Believers are to beware of unbelievers ways and to do all they can to help them see the light.

Church as Public School. Gathered worship is a place for uniform instruction and formation. The truth is clearly taught and what a well-discipled individual will look like is known from the outset.

Mission as Winning Debates or Clients. God's calling is to contend for the gospel. Christians do well to learn to share and defend their faith effectively. The unsaved are potential recruits for the community.

Judgment as Apt Punishment for Breaking the Rules. God longs for all people to come to repentance, yet, he is holy. All will be punished for their transgressions if they do not ask for forgiveness.

> Wherever I look for the roots of modernity, I find it in attempts of the churches to institutionalize and manage Christian vocation.
>
> —Ivan Illich[5]

5. Cayley, *Rivers North of the Future*, 48.

Secular Faith:

The world without Christ contains echoes of Divine intention, and yet the original image is severely cracked. No person is without some truth. No individual is evil all the way through. Yet, open-minded Christians may want to be careful about throwing out the Christian baby with the dirty church bath water. True, the "secular" vision is different from contemporary Christianity in many ways. But I fear the freedom it offers is a Trojan horse. Standing straight next to the assumptions and values of the larger contemporary culture can also weary the bones.

When *I* read and experience contemporary American culture, these phrases and descriptions rise up into *my* vision:

> *God as a Fantasy or Irrelevancy.* God may or may not exist. Who really knows? What matters is finding a life that works, satisfies, and doesn't hurt other people.

> *Theological Truth as Superstition.* Clearly, ancient people did not know what we know. What they believed as divine revelation was a mix of naïve hunches and bad science.

> *The Bible as Myths from an Undeveloped People.* The Bible does contain many interesting stories and some helpful suggestions on how to treat other people. But it has largely been proven false as the imagination of uneducated forbearers.

> *Spirituality as Finding Oneself.* Spirituality is helpful. It is a healthy thing to know thyself: your deepest values and dreams, and to find motivational methods of working towards these aspirations.

> *Faith as Positive Thinking.* It is far better to be hopeful than negative. It is more desirable to see the bright side than the downside. Faith is simply believing that a better day lies ahead.

> *The Arts as an Entertaining Consumable.* Life can be challenging and stressful. Watching a film or attending a concert can bring a little fun to a down week.

> *The Entrapment of the Everyday.* To be ordinary, is to be unnoticed. The common has no punch. To be mainstream is to be irrelevant. Do everything you can to be extraordinary.

Human Beings as Independent Consuming Machines. Men and women, boys and girls, have the right to be and pursue whatever they desire. We are primarily led by biological impulses and it is unhealthy to suppress our truest longings.

Church as Political Action Committee. Churches are collections of conservative and traditional people who may mean well, but who are mainly bent on controlling society.

Mission as Brainwashing. Believing something to the point of working to convince others is an act of intrusion and existential violence.

Judgment as Hateful Rhetoric. To think that anyone will end up on the wrong side of eternity is a dangerous belief that is the source of all kinds of cruelty and psychological pathology.

Again, I have little doubt that a trained theologian or historian would be able to point out all sorts of over-simplifications with my understanding of premodern Christianity. Not to mention my overly crude generalization of contemporary faith and secular narratives. Certainly there are a myriad of interpretations for any historical epoch, without even mentioning all of the varied points of view that exist within any time and place. There is no such thing as "the" premodern Christianity. There would have been as many variations of organized Christian thought and practice as there are within our current age.

But that is not my point.

What I am trying to highlight is that there are *other* ways of being truly orthodox (as opposed to heretical or re-invented) besides the contemporary forms of American Christianity that feel too stuffy, stale, and tightly packaged. The odd allure that C. S. Lewis generated in the 1940s was the direct result of him drinking from the stream at a different point in the flow. Lewis and others like him did not reinvent the faith. He did anything but make things up according to personal whims and inclinations. He gladly embraced all the essential tenets of the faith: the Triune Creator, the inherit worth and yet sinfulness of humanity, the inspiration of the Scriptures, the virgin birth, the deity of Christ, His atoning death for the benefit of humanity, His bodily resurrection, saving faith, the eschaton, etc.

Yet because Lewis drank from the water upstream, his vision and understanding of orthodox faith was not the same thing as our contemporary assumptions. In Sweet's words, he "leaned all the way back."

> But that's only half of what he was doing.
>
>> We all want progress. But progress means getting nearer to the place where you want to be. And if you have taken a wrong turning then to go forward does not get you any nearer. If you are on the wrong road progress means doing an about-turn and walking back to the right road and in that case the man who turns back soonest is the most progressive man.
>>
>> —C. S. Lewis[6]

Kicking Forward

What made C. S. Lewis the most effective apologist in the twentieth century (and what can make him feel slightly crusty today) is that he leaned all the way back for his theological vision and yet, he kicked forward using the cutting edge communicative techniques of his day.

But Lewis was not the only one to do so.

Leonard Sweet claims that he has a relationship with Jesus and with John Wesley. The founder of Methodism stood out in the eighteenth century as an amazingly innovative messenger of the gospel. His Arminianism was in the clear minority in a thick culture of European Reformed Christianity. His style of open-air preaching to the masses was shocking to the church establishment. His detractors thought of him as wildly reckless in thought and form. Yet, the staying power of Spirit-filled life-change, experienced by so many of the masses, speaks of his truly being on to something.

What did Wesley do? He leaned all the way back, drawing much of his theology from the Eastern Church Fathers (premodern orthodoxy). While simultaneously kicking forward by studying contemporary culture and following out the communicative implications for the working masses in burgeoning industrial England.

Wesley recognized (like Lewis and Sweet) that Enlightenment inspired theology gutted the mystery, the inspiration, the layered and imaginatively redemptive qualities of speaking and living after a Living God. Paradoxically, he discerned that traditional forms of communication did not make sense, nor appear attractive, to the common man and woman of his day.

Using C. S. Lewis and John Wesley as historical examples, I offer the simple proposal:

---

6. Lewis, *Mere Christianity*, 36.

Signs of the Times

*Premodern orthodoxy + contemporary communication
= refreshing and life-challenging ministry.*

This is what it means to "lean all the way back and to kick forward."

I have shared my personal story, vision, and interpretation of Sweet's call to the church. The obvious question then becomes "What do I do with this as a ministry leader?" Leonard Sweet has provided countless ministers with much heady fodder to consider. But many of his readers are left scratching their head asking what it all means.

All ministry is local. Every specific manifestation of the Spirit and kingdom will be unique. But below are some tangible ways of leaning back and kicking forward as you roll up your sleeves and seek to minister to others.

View Yourself as a Missionary

Assuming it's true that premodern orthodoxy contains neglected elements of truly following Christ, then we are more like missionaries than pastors. These are two different understandings of vocation.

Pastors primarily see themselves as examples of holiness and piety for believers. They encourage the flock and see to it that budgets and buildings are cared for. Pastoring is important, but it's only valued within traditional communities.

Missionaries know that they are marginal to society. They know their beliefs are radically different from those they are sent to reach. They have to experiment with bridge-building. Trying on different customs, and practices, and languages. Missionaries never assume they will somehow become just like those they are ministering to. They know, if I dare say so, they are clandestine, resident aliens to the host culture.

And maybe you should know that too?

> The world into which the first Christians carried the gospel was a religiously plural world and—as the letters of Paul show—in that world of many lords and many gods, Christians had to work out what it means that in fact Jesus alone is Lord.
>
> —Lesslie Newbigin[7]

---

7. Newbigin, *Gospel in a Pluralist Society*, 157.

Recognize That Everyone Comes from a Faith Commitment

It can be chic today in our public communication to dis "religion." Many pastors, trying to build bridges, have used the phrase "It's not a religion, it's a relationship." Maybe for some this works.

But woe to us if we operate as if people's options are:

1. Faith

or

2. No faith.

Everyone comes from a faith commitment. To assume that one is not religious is to be blinded to the reality that one has completely converted to the religion of the dominant culture.

The freedom of the individual.

Separation of church and state.

Pursuing one's dreams.

Emancipation from other's dogmatisms.

The free market.

Representative democracy.

The American Dream.

Historical progress.

Education and technology as keys to the future.

These are ALL *theological statements of a religion.*

Contemporary American secularism is built on faith commitments. It has a pope: the democratically elected president. It has bishops and priests: entertainers and corporate leaders. It has seminaries: public universities. It has a catechism: public schools. It has prophets: the mass media. It has a list of deadly sins: political correctness. It has a gospel: individual freedom and mass consumption. It has a church: the shopping mall (or Amazon.) It has the damned: the economically deprived. It has a new heavens and earth: technological and medical advancements.

It is probably bad form to baldly name these. But a wise missionary understands the religion of those they are seeking to reach.

Exegete your culture: watch the movies; listen to different Pandora stations, read several blogs. But most importantly, listen to the natives. And note: they are *not* without faith. They are pious adherents of secular, Western, democratic, individualism. This *is* a religion.

> In a society which has exulted the autonomous individual as the supreme reality, we are accustomed to the rich variety offered on the supermarket shelves and to the freedom we have to choose our favorite brands. It is very natural that this mentality should pervade our view of religion.
>
> —*Lesslie Newbigin*[8]

> The god most Americans say they believe in . . . is only the god that has given them a country that ensures that they have the right to choose to believe in the god of their choosing. Accordingly, the only kind of atheism that counts in the US is that which calls into question the proposition that everyone has a right to life, liberty, and happiness.
>
> —*Stanley Hauerwas*[9]

Look for Those Disenfranchised with the Secular Religion

Missionaries do not tend to reach those who are thriving within a host culture and its religious system. Those who are satisfied with what is, are rarely seeking what could be.

In twenty-first-century America, it is doubtful that you will be effective with those who are reasonably well off, who have plenty of family and friends nearby, who have moderately stable relationships, who are physically healthy. Chasing them is rarely following the Spirit.

But those who struggling in an economic vice, those who are new to the area and don't know anyone, those who are recently divorced or coming off of a bad break-up, those who deal with physical ailments, these may just be the ones who are questioning the religious faith of the American Dream that they were raised in.

To be accepted by the happy, healthy, and networked usually requires morphing faith in Jesus into the faith of the current secular age.

---

8. Ibid., 168.

9. Hauerwas, *How Real Is America's Faith?*

To be interesting to the struggling, the sick, and the lonely requires simply telling a very different story. Look for them—that's where you will find the Spirit's work.

Learn to Tell a Better Story

Rational proofs have very little "pop" in a secular culture of choice. Highly reasoned out defenses of Christianity is playing the game of secularism. People who insist on evidence and logical arguments are incapable of simultaneously catching the Spirit.

But an explanation of life that is more hopeful, more meaningful, and resonant can be compelling. Telling a better story helps to name their "story" for what it truly is.

I have had a number of friends over the years that not only disbelieve in the Triune God of Scripture; they find it highly unlikely that any sort of Divine Creator exists at all.

They tell a story something like this: "Look, any half-way educated and sane individual knows that no one is out there. 'God' exists only for those who need some hope outside of themselves. Those who are struggling to survive. Like those poor souls who live in third-world squalor. Those who are without education or opportunity living in the forgotten recesses of Appalachia. The rest of us understand that God does not exist. We don't need him. He's an idea for those who need motivation to keep going and to keep doing the right thing when it feels like everything is about to fall apart."

I admit that there certainly is some truth in this story. Many who live reasonably happy and affluent lives see little utility in committed faith. And of course it is true, that those who consistently face the threat of death are much more open to the reality and potential benefits of serious spiritually and traditional beliefs.

Historically speaking, the Christian story does emphasize that the new heavens and the new earth will be an embodied existence with no more pain, tears, suffering, and loss. The renewed creation is where grieving mothers will be reunited with dead children. Where those who perished due to malnourishment, will feast at the grand banquet of plenty. Where injustice is not even a faint memory, and all of humanity will experience a community of love and joy. It is a very different story.

What many of my skeptical friends often fail to notice though, is just how ugly, depressing, and potentially unjust their story can be. They forget that they are 1 percent-ers. That they are part of the all-too-privileged few in the West with higher educations, with good salaries, with state-of-the-art healthcare, those whose biggest physical problem is deciding what to select off of today's lunch menu. The vast majority of people who have ever lived, who live today all over the globe, know what is like to go days without food, to bury a one year old due to inadequate nourishment, to experience dysentery as a regular part of the human condition.

If one were to adopt the Christian story, well then, these millions and billions of souls who suffer throughout their days have the potential of truly experiencing a happy ending. A time of literal resurrection. A glorious future.

But if we adopted the skeptics' narrative, well then, these millions and billions of people suffer throughout their days and will find no ultimate sense of meaning. The mother who mourns for a child truly has no hope. A man who struggles under severe illness and slave-like conditions will never be freed. Even more, those one-tenth of 1 percent-ers, those shrewd folks who live in McMansions and spend their earnings on private educations and plastic surgery, well, they are the smart ones. They are the victors. This life is all there is and they are making the most of it. They have figured out how to live pleasurably, and what else could one look forward to?

What is a better story?

> [Secularism] is only a mythos, and therefore cannot be refuted, but only out-narrated, if we can persuade people—for reasons of "literary taste"—that Christianity offers a much better story.
>
> —John Milbank[10]

Conclusion

It has never been easy to serve in the ministry, but it has probably never been more complex. Western economies are rapidly morphing and leaving most behind. Civil society is quickly fragmenting, fostering more divisiveness and confusion. Ethics and morality are increasingly evaporating, leaving every person powerless against his or her own passions and consuming desires.

---

10. Milbank, *Theology and Social Theory*, 331.

The weather is changing and the waves of the seas are threatening to grow into unnavigable swells. If this were not the case, there never would have been a Leonard Sweet.

But he cannot pilot the ship for you. And of course, he doesn't know how to navigate every storm that the wind may carry along. But his sailing lessons have served me well.

Don't think an anchored ship can save you. You will be dead in the water. Conservative, contemporary Evangelicalism will hold you still when it may be safer to navigate the ship along to a safer port.

Don't think you can survive adrift in the currents. You will capsize or smash against the rocks. Enjoying brief popularity, by joining the values and beliefs of our secular age, will sink you in the end.

Look forward and see what is appearing new on the horizon, while leaning back and keeping a hand on the rudder of the Christian past. You may sail east or west at times. You may not feel like you are advancing in every day of the ministry. But eventually, you will find your way home.

> Live with your century, but do not be its captive; render to your contemporaries what they need, not what they praise.
>
> —*Friedrich Schiller*[11]

Bibliography

Burke, Spencer. *Making Sense of Church*. Grand Rapids: Zondervan, 2003.
Cayley, David, ed. *The Rivers North of the Future: The Testament of Ivan Illich as Told to David Cayley*. Toronto: House of Anansi, 2005.
Chesterton, G. K. *Orthodoxy*. New York: Image (Doubleday), 2001.
Hauerwas, Stanley. "How Real Is America's Faith?" *Guardian*, October 16, 2010. http://www.theguardian.com/commentisfree/belief/2010/oct/16/faith-america-secular-britain.
Horton, Scott. "Schiller's Rules of Engagement." *Browsings* (*Harper's* blog), November 8, 2008. http://harpers.org/blog/2008/11/schillers-rules-of-engagement.
Lewis, C. S. *Mere Christianity*. New York: Simon & Schuster, 1996.
Milbank, John. *Theology and Social Theory: Beyond Secular Reason*. Malden, MA: Blackwell, 2006.
Newbigin, Lesslie. *The Gospel in a Pluralist Society*. Grand Rapids: Eerdmans, 2001.
Staub, Dick. *The Culturally Savvy Christian: A Manifesto for Deepening Faith and Enriching Popular Culture in an Age of Christianity-Lite*. San Francisco: Jossey-Bass, 2008.
Sweet, Leonard, et al. *A Is for Abductive: The Language of the Emerging Church*. Grand Rapids: Zondervan, 2003.

---

11. Horton, "Schiller's Rules of Engagement."

13

Reading the Signs
Serving Families Affected by Disability

Christine Roush, DMin

"Ok, now don't look in the rearview mirror. Tell me what is back there behind you." For my driver's ed teacher it was a favorite game. For months he had been teaching us to pay attention to the world around us, including cars approaching from behind. "You have to be observant," he would say. "You should always know what's back there. Who is coming up fast? Who is getting ready to pass? Watch the car about to enter your blind spot, and then don't forget they are there. *Pay attention*"! Since my friends and I rarely *were* noticing what was going on behind us, the game was kind of fun.

Unless you were the driver he was focusing on!

That driver's education class taught me to notice the world around me. At the age of seventeen, I had no idea that this concept—intentionally noticing the world around me—would hold such meaning for me in my ministry. Ministry today challenges us to pay attention. It requires us to read the signs of the lives of the people we encounter each day.

I learned some great ministry lessons on class road trips with Leonard Sweet. "Who did you see?" he would ask. "Were they alone? Did they look happy? Were they enjoying a conversation? What signs did you see?" There had been a family at dinner. No one seemed to be talking. Waiting, it seemed. It did not appear like there was a lot of joy to be found at that table. Another corner of the restaurant had two tables against the wall, one person sitting at each of them. Both looked lonely, ill at ease to be eating by themselves at a table for four. A smiling waitress stood nearby, looking like today was a good day for her. At another table sat a woman looking weary and struggling to keep ahead of three small children. She was not wearing a wedding ring.

It's amazing what you see when you actually pay attention—when you read the signs.

We live in arguably one of the most stressed-out, overworked, self-centered cultures on the planet. Preoccupied with our own problems and agendas, few of us find time to ever take note of the people around us—to read the signs plainly captured on their faces. Some of us are even so busy saving the world for Christ, we sometimes inadvertently walk right past the very ones the Lord has called us to serve!

That's the problem with listening to Leonard Sweet. He leads you to question what often goes overlooked. When it comes to measuring success, he challenged me to wonder if God uses the same kind of measure society uses. When I look around my world, *really look*, I see a lot of hurting individuals. I see women and men desperate for someone to sit down and listen to them. I see single moms trying to hold life together with too little money or help. I see lonely seniors who have lost their mate, hoping somebody will take the time to have a cup of coffee and listen to a story or two. I see teens working their way through their awkward stage, desperately trying to find a way to fit in. I see foster kids and children with disabilities. I see families crushed by poverty and communities torn apart by racism. If you hang around Leonard Sweet too long, you will find yourself reading the signs and paying closer attention to what they tell you about individual people. The message is clear—we live in a world desperate for the good news. As ministry leaders, God expects us to find ways to shine the light of Christ into their pain.

Once I started to pay attention to what I was seeing, the focus of my ministry shifted. Sign reading led me down two paths. First, my perception switched from actions that were preserving the church as an institution, to focusing on individuals with their own stories—their hurts and needs. Second, I started searching for what Jesus was already doing outside the walls of his church, and looked for places where I could join him. God eventually led me to the world of disability ministries. For me, that is where all the pieces began to fall in place.

When you look at the church in your community, what do you see? When I began to purposefully observe the local churches around me, I saw a sea of change. Churches were getting smaller and older. Both leadership and their congregations were growing more entrenched, less open to creativity and change. Youth were disappearing, and while churches bemoaned their loss, few attempted the steps necessary to give those who were leaving any real reason to stay. The actions of many congregations and their leaders spoke louder than their words. The message was clear. *"Come on in! We are friendly, caring people who welcome folks! However . . . we like this church exactly how it is so don't ask us to change anything."* Even the pastors most determined to lead their congregations into new patterns, were growing exhausted from pushing against the currents of tradition and entrenched lay leadership.

Outside of the church, the signs are equally disturbing. We live in one of the most affluent societies that has ever existed. Yet despite this, our rates of depression, suicide, anxiety and isolation continue to climb.[1] People feel alone and without hope—however statistics indicate that few see the church as a helpful resource in their search for answers.[2] For some people, the church seems focused on shoring up an institution, yet spends little time with people who are in deep need of simply being loved. Others perceive Christians as judgmental, hypocritical, old-fashioned and anti-homosexual.[3]

My personal analysis of these signs led to a calling to focus on people as individuals with their own hopes and dreams; with their own unique joys and sorrows. I was invited to work at a "high touch" residential ministry working with adults with developmental disabilities: Rainbow Acres in Camp Verde, Arizona. This calling challenged every perception I previously held about what it means to be a pastor, and even, what it means to be a person of faith. Right away I witnessed God at work at Rainbow Acres. It is a community where every individual is treated with dignity and respect. Almost immediately, I also saw the incredible need in our world for church families, everywhere, to walk alongside family members affected by a child or a sibling with a disability.

Through the ministry at Rainbow Acres, I began to see opportunities for serving as the hands of Christ in ways that could breathe new life into people and churches. The hands-on, individualized, personal ministry of serving people with disabilities and their families has the potential to remind every active participant of what it means to be Christ to a hurting

---

1. Myers, *American Paradox*, 161–94.
2. Kinnaman, *You Lost Me*, 92–93.
3. Barna, "New Generation Expresses Its Skepticism."

world. Ministry within the disabilities community requires far more than a new program or a budget line. It takes an investment of time, compassion and attention. Investing in ministry with families touched by disability, can give meaning to not only the families served, but it can also bring a congregation back to its roots—loving our neighbors as Christ has taught us to love them.

So here are two simple questions. Is it possible that we made living our faith far more complicated than God ever desired? Can the mission of a church be as simple as loving God and loving people?

When it comes to working with people with disabilities, how the church decides to answer these two questions is critical. It all comes down to attention and focus. Worried about political agendas, choosing between singing praise songs or hymns, or chasing after whoever borrowed the tables out of the youth room, leaves little time for ministry serving people with physical or developmental disabilities.

The church, the community where we teach that everyone is a precious child created in the likeness of God, is often missing in action when it comes to people with disabilities. We the people of the great stories of Christ showing compassion and mercy—Jesus interacting with the blind man, the beggar at the gate, the man who could not walk, the woman who touched the Lord's robe for healing—rarely interact with individuals and families affected by disability. Focused on our own congregations and agendas, we miss millions of individuals and families desperately looking for relationships laced with caring and compassion.

> Are we spending our lives on ourselves? Are we the center of our universe? Or do we deny ourselves in the name of Christ. Every commercial, every message says you are the center of the world. It is the original sin—you are God.
>
> —*Leonard Sweet*[4]

The church world tells us it is perfectly normal to focus on the people already in our pews. Tragically, this self-centered view of life continues to enable followers of Christ to ignore some of the people most in need of hearing his good news.

---

4. Leonard Sweet, in discussion with the author, May 2007.

The Mission Field Is At Hand

The facts are stark. According to the Center for Disease Control (CDC), one in eighty-eight children born in the United States today will struggle with autism, and about one in six children have some particular type of a developmental disability. A Cornell University study, utilizing the 2011 US Census Bureau's American Community Survey, places the total number of Americans with a disability at an estimated 12 percent of the population.[5]

If there were ever a time to read the signs, it is today. Few situations create more hopelessness, more anxiety and stress, or more of a sense of isolation, than raising a child with a disability. Days and weeks of testing and appointments with specialists, turn into months and years of struggling with figuring out how to keep life together. Advocating for your child becomes a way of life, an art form. You watch other children work their way through developmental stages you only dream about. Simple tasks like learning to speak, or how to tie shoe laces, become minor miracles within your home. The grief of what will never be a possibility for your child—eventually gets replaced by the grief of watching your child become isolated and left behind. The cruelty of thoughtless comments and demeaning stares leave devastating wounds.

> It ain't those parts of the Bible that I can't understand that bother me, it's the parts that I do understand.
>
> —Mark Twain

When it comes to people with disabilities, two of the easiest messages ever preached by Leonard Sweet—read the signs and WIJD (What Is Jesus Doing)—seem to highlight the truth of Twain's words. It's not the complicated things that are the most difficult for us as leaders to wrap our minds around. It is the simple messages. The need for the good news of Jesus Christ to be experienced within the disabilities community is clear. The signs are all around us:

- Adults with a developmental disability are eight times more likely to be abused than the average person.[6]

---

5. Erickson et al., *2011 Disability Status Report*.
6. See Bethesda Institute, *Abuse and Neglect*.

- Nearly one in five adults with a developmental disability live in poverty.[7]
- Adults with developmental disabilities face lives of isolation. Parents of potential residents at Rainbow Acres regularly admit, "I just want my son/daughter to have friends."
- The financial and emotional pressures are enormous on families of persons with disabilities.[8]
- Seventy-nine percent of people with disabilities face chronic unemployment or under employment. A 2010 survey by the National Organization on Disability indicated only 21 percent held a part-time or full-time job.[9]
- According to Calvin College and Seminary's Institute of Christian Worship, more than 80 percent of people with disabilities don't attend church.[10]

Perhaps most discouraging, adults with disabilities may actually be losing some of the gains made in recent years as a result of the Americans with Disabilities Act. The executive summary of the 2010 survey, conducted by the Kessler Foundation and the National Organization on Disability, concluded:

> While there has been modest improvement among a few indicators, the general trend of the measures is that twenty years after the passage of the Americans with Disabilities Act (ADA), there has yet to be significant progress in many areas. For instance, although there has been substantial improvement reported in education attainment and political participation since 1986, large gaps still exist between people with and without disabilities with regard to: employment, household income, access to transportation, health care, socializing, going to restaurants, and satisfaction with life. *In some instances, the spread has actually gotten worse since the inception of the survey in 1986.*[11]

---

7. "Nearly 1 in 5 People Have a Disability in the U.S.," Census.gov news release, July 25, 2012, http://www.census.gov/newsroom/releases/archives/miscellaneous/cb12-134.html.

8. See Easter Seals, *Siblings Study*.

9. Taylor et al., "ADA, 20 Years Later," 7.

10. Huyser-Honig, "All God's Children Have Gifts."

11. Taylor et al., "ADA, 20 Years Later," 5 (emphasis added).

So how *does* a church attempt to be Christ for the disabilities community? How do we figure out what Jesus is already doing, and jump on board?

The Road Less Traveled (Churches Who Have Chosen to Make a Difference)

> "What would Jesus do"? is not Christianity. Christianity asks: "What is Christ doing through me . . . through us? And how is Jesus doing it"? Following Jesus means "trust and obey" (respond), and living by his indwelling life through the power of the Spirit."
>
> —*Leonard Sweet and Frank Viola*[12]

Getting started: The first step in any ministry is to start by recognizing there is a need. In the case of disability ministries, that's easy! Autism rates are so prevalent virtually every church has a family who has been touched by the spectrum of autism disorders, Down's syndrome, or some other form of intellectual disability.

In terms of working with people with disabilities, the *real* challenge may be twofold. First, it will be necessary to overcome fear and misconceptions. It is critical to begin seeing these individuals as people—not as someone with a disability. Despite our differences, most of us have more in common with each other than we often recognize. There is a basic human longing for friendship, a chance to contribute, and to be seen as an individual who is worthy of dignity and respect. We are all beloved children of God! Whether locked in a wheelchair, wrestling with the involuntary movements of cerebral palsy, grinning with the childlike joy of an adult with Down's syndrome, or walking with the telltale white cane of the blind—we all have the same hopes and dreams. We all simply long for friends and a place where we feel as though we belong.

Begin at the Beginning—Seeing People, Not Disabilities

For the purposes of this chapter, the primary form of disability discussed will be those of a cognitive/developmental nature. However, physical disabilities can prove to be an equal barrier to inclusion within a church. I recently learned about a young couple who had been attending a church

---

12. Sweet, "Magna Carta."

faithfully for nearly a year. Both blind, their families had associations within the church and so they had hoped to also become a part of the faith community. When they were absent for a number of weeks the pastor stopped by to see how they were doing. "We are fine," the young man relayed. "We just got tired of people behaving as if we are not there. I may be blind, but I can hear with no problem. I know people are sitting near me, walking by me, and talking to folks right next to me, yet no one says anything to us. Why do we want to keep going someplace where no one besides the pastor seems to care if we are there?"

Wheelchairs can have a similar affect. Did you ever notice how people react to someone in a wheelchair? Very rarely do they look the person in the eye. Sure, this probably comes from our attempts to be polite. We were taught not to stare. In our efforts to not be offensive, however, we border on not even acknowledging that the other person exists! As people of faith, seeing someone in a wheelchair as *first*, a person, and *second*, as someone in a wheelchair, is a great place to start.

Years ago a woman in the camp where I served used a motorized wheelchair to get around. The first time I actually noticed her, I was focused on how she was making her way into our dining hall and I was not engaging her as an individual. I watched as her family walked with her up the ramp and into the back door of our main lodge. Since the back door was adjacent to our main dumpster—we had clearly given little thought to the dignity of people who would need to use this route! Eventually, it seemed demeaning to me. I decided that we should build a new ramp into the front door of our dining hall to address the problem. The next year when she came back, I had decided to approach her to see how she liked the new entry way.

Her body frequently shifted within her chair and the keyboard in front of her signaled her struggles to communicate. Though I had no idea what her disabilities were, I made some assumptions about how the conversation might go before I ever sat down and introduced myself. They were all wrong. When I took time to actually engage her in a conversation, I discovered a brilliant mind locked inside a body that simply wouldn't cooperate. To connect, I only had to show interest in her as a person, and to wait patiently as she willed her fingers toward the correct letters on the keyboard. I discovered she was an accomplished writer and had published several articles on the difficulties associated with disability. She taught me a great deal. Probably the most critical lesson I learned from that experience was this: being Christ in her life was as simple as sitting down and having a conversation. Through personal time spent with her, I no longer saw her as a woman with a disability or a woman in a wheelchair. Instead, I saw her as a person with hopes, dreams, gifts and skills. Someone whom I really enjoyed getting to know. *But I had to make time for the conversation first!*

People frequently treat the disabilities community with "helicopter interactions." Swoop in, swoop out—there! This is not truly being present . . . Swooping in and swooping out is not interaction, or connection, or human engagement.

My friend in the wheelchair at camp has been a victim of the failure to connect with people with special needs. People would often say hi and keep walking. She would try to frantically tap out a response in the hopes of having a *real* conversation before a passerby would leave. Her disability meant she hit a lot of wrong keys in this mad dash to be heard. When I brought a cup of coffee over, pulled out the chair beside her, and made it clear I was hanging around for some time, her movements slowed. The extra time reduced her anxiety, and she typed with a great deal more accuracy. How sad that the simple act of trying to respond to a "hello" was often so rushed for her that it added to her sense of failure and isolation. Taking time to spend a few minutes and actually *get to know someone* can be the most precious gift of all.

Take time to get to know the people with disabilities in your community. Read the signs! They have stories to share. There are joys and pains, hopes and dreams, just waiting to be heard and understood.

I have to admit that I entered the world of adults with intellectual disabilities skeptical about how God could use me. Though not fearful, I could not see any real connection between my gifts and ministry within the field of disability. Having been actively involved as a denominational staff member in camping, field ministry and mission promotion, intersection with adults with traumatic brain injury, serving people with Down's syndrome or intellectual disability, was not an immediately obvious next ministry for me. But I sat down to lunch on my first visit to Rainbow Acres and quickly realized that I had been eating with these folks for most of my career. They sat at every middle school lunch table I had ever joined while teaching or serving at summer camp. Topics ranged from who was dating who, to what was on TV the night before. I instantly felt right at home.

What misconceptions keep *you* from building friendships with people with disabilities within your own community? What beliefs stand in *your* way?

I'd like to suggest you consider a shift in your perspective. When it comes to adults with developmental disabilities, looks can be deceiving. Our mind tells us what we should expect—they look like a grown up, surely they will behave as a grown up does. But they can't.

Did you ever notice that it is okay to be a five-year-old in a five-year-old body, or a twelve-year-old in a twelve-year-old body—yet as a society, we have no clue what to do with a five-year-old in a fifty-year-old body? Adults with developmental disabilities are often kids wearing an adult body. Though they look fully developed, and society expects them to act as adults, they cannot function according to our expectations. They are not wired that way. But once you start looking for that childlike response instead of the adult one—you will find some amazing people hidden inside. It is really all about your perspective. Our residents at Rainbow Acres are some of the funniest, kindest, most caring people I have ever met. I just had to look past the adult body and search for the child hidden inside.

Then What?

Ministries to families affected by disability can take dozens of forms—and they are all desperately needed! In the immortal words of Nike—just do it! Every church and community is different, and each will have its own unique set of circumstances determining the best way forward. You can begin by asking a couple people with a passion for persons with disabilities to get together with you and talk about what is needed in your community. If local needs are not immediately obvious, try soliciting input from your local school system or a nearby group home or program for adults with developmental disabilities. Special education teachers, parents or grandparents of children or adults with disabilities, medical personnel, and adults who have a developmental disability themselves, could all be potential members of a quick brain storming session with valuable input for what direction your ministry could take.

I was invited to serve on a panel a few years ago at a church. The pastor was exploring with his congregation the topic of marginalized people. That night they were focusing on developmental disabilities, and since I worked with adults with disabilities every day, I was invited to participate in the conversation. Two other members of the panel were parents of adult men, one with a traumatic brain injury, and the other with autism.

"How could the church have served you when your son was growing up?" the pastor asked. One mother responded instantly, "I would have liked them to welcome us. We never felt like we were wanted. Our son had a hard time sitting still. At times, he was noisy. No church ever encouraged us to get involved. They wanted me to come, or my husband to come; but they didn't want us to come together because they didn't want my son there. One church even asked us to not come back. We felt really alone, like social outcasts."

Ministry to families affected by disability can be as simple as welcoming them. I wish I could adequately express the deep pain that was evident in the both the words and the facial expression of the mother who shared on the panel that evening. At a time in their lives when they needed God, friends, and help most—they could not find a church that would welcome them. Helping them to feel a part of the church community could have happened in a variety of ways. Weekly phone calls just to check in, a support group for parents, a mom's night out once or twice a year—any attempt would have felt like Christ to her in that time of pain. What could your church do for those in your community feeling just like this mom did?

Some Ideas

Incorporate diversity into worship. Many congregations successfully include people with disabilities into the ordinary life of the church. They understand an adult with a developmental disability is like a child in a fifty year old body, and set their expectations accordingly. No question asked in a sermon can be assumed rhetorical, and the pastor understands they may get an actual answer for every hypothetical question they pose. If your congregation is open, persons with disabilities can be included as candle lighters, greeters, ushers, and members of the choir and drama group. Involving persons with cognitive disabilities in worship can be a wonderful way to model the diversity of the body of Christ!

Special services for persons with disabilities can also work well. Leaving time for a separate, more laid-back service, at the same time the children step out can be effective, but it does require some church leaders to miss the morning message as well. Remember—if a preteen would like this special service—probably your adults with developmental disabilities will like it too. If you are unsure, *just ask them*! Like many children and the elderly, they are happy to clearly share the truth of how they feel if you ask them!

I'd encourage you, though, to not assume people with disabilities won't sit through a normal worship service. Many have jobs that require their patience and attention. Others simply enjoy being part of the community, and they act just like everyone else. If it is an interesting service, they will be just as actively engaged as all the other worship participants. (And if it is not an interesting service, well they are probably not the only ones who will be struggling!)

A *monthly small group for parents*, along with *a very well-staffed* activity for children with disabilities and their siblings, can be another helpful idea. Parents need time to talk and often to grieve with other families who are struggling with similar realities. Sharing with others going through the same issues can be a tremendous gift. Plan appropriate activities to keep a variety of ages busy, and assume you will need one-on-one care for at least a couple of your families.

Provide for *occasional weekend respite care*. Parents of one of our residents here at Rainbow Acres shared that in over twenty-seven years, they had been away from their son for a total of two weekends. No wonder holding marriages together is such a difficult task for couples with a child with a disability.[13] With the birth of a special-needs child, parents experience the pain and sadness of lost hopes and dreams. Combined with all the financial distress and the challenges of specialist appointments and routine care, couples never have time alone to focus on their marriage. Consider finding ways to help couples get a break. You can accomplish this through discovering qualified, licensed and approved caregivers within your congregation and arranging a weekend away, by covering the costs of a certified respite facility (think summer camp or weekend get-away designed for the special-needs population) or even by helping fund an extended family member's trip to come stay with the child or adult enabling parents to take a mini vacation alone. You might try taking a special offering to assist with the costs of respite care for the couple or the family. While most members of your church would not be able to serve as respite caregivers, many will want to help. An offering can give them the opportunity to show their support in a meaningful way.

When I discovered the numbers of families who were bringing their child with special needs to camp for a week and taking the rest of the family on vacation somewhere else, a light bulb came on for me. At first offended on behalf of the child left behind, I came to understand just how important

---

13. See Harper et al., "Respite Care."

it was for these families to be able to spend a week focusing on their other children. After spending all their young lives in the shadow of the overwhelming needs of their siblings with special needs, those youngsters deserved all of Mom and Dad's attention for one week too! Perhaps your church could consider a *special-needs Vacation Bible School* where families can do fun activities with the siblings while you help do something their special-needs child would enjoy. It can be a win for both. A Vacation Bible School, especially for them, will keep the kids with disabilities *and* their siblings from getting lost in the shuffle.

(A word of caution. This segregation needs to be for the right reasons. These children and youth are already left with the impression they don't belong in much of what happens in their lives. Other children at school probably let them know they are different with alarming frequency. Doing a special VBS so you can focus on them is great. Doing it separately so as to not "burden the rest of your kids" is not!)

Monthly small group for adults with developmental disabilities. Just like all your other small groups, a group focused specifically for adults with developmental disabilities can be greatly appreciated. Program it just like you would a middle school function. Provide cookies or snacks, and trust me—they will come. Adults with developmental disabilities could easily be folded into existing small groups if done intentionally. Just make sure they are made to feel welcome. A mom once shared with me that her daughter refused to go to a small group, after attending three or four previous gatherings with no problem. When she asked her daughter why she wanted to stay home, her answer was simple. "No one ever talks to me." Even cake and ice cream is not enough to keep you coming if you don't feel a part of the group.

Go to them. One of the newest movements within the disabilities community is to eliminate institutional-type settings in favor of a smaller group home. While the intent was not without merit (shutting down large, uncaring institutions) the solution was not necessarily a perfect one. The purpose was to mainstream adults with disabilities into our communities. However, in many instances it has largely resulted in isolating the group home residents in the midst of neighbors. Few communities have embraced group homes in their areas.

Your church can change that! Make the residents of these homes in your neighborhood a part of your care circle. Invite them to church, but also talk to the caregivers and find out how you can practically be like

Christ for them. Get to know them and their caregivers by going to their home. Try joining them for dinner, taking them to a movie, or shopping for a birthday gift with them. Any activity to help them feel a part of the community would be appreciated.

A Final Word

The need to experience the good news of Jesus Christ within the disabilities community is overwhelming. Any attempt to move forward with God in this direction is a positive development. From sensitizing our church families about the importance of treating people with disabilities as individuals, to launching large-scale ministries for families affected by disability—each and every attempt has the potential to help Christ come alive for individuals and families dealing with disability. Ministry really *can* be this simple—loving people, including people with disabilities—the way we want to be loved ourselves. Find the places where Christ is already at work and get involved. Become the hands and feet of Christ for the families with disabilities in your community today!

Bibliography

Barna. "A New Generation Expresses Its Skepticism and Frustration with Christianity." *Barna.org*, September 21, 2007. https://www.barna.org/barna-update/millennials/94-a-new-generation-expresses-its-skepticism-and-frustration-with-christianity#.VoEHDPkrLIU.

Bethesda Institute. *Abuse and Neglect*. DVD. 33 mins. Staff training material.

Easter Seals. *Siblings Study*. Easter Seals Disability Services. www.easterseals.com/explore-resources/siblings-study.html.

Erickson, W., et al. *2011 Disability Status Report United States*. Employment and Disability Institute, Cornell University ILR School, 2012. http://www.disabilitystatistics.org/StatusReports/2011-PDF/2011-StatusReport_US.pdf.

Harper, Amber, et al. "Respite Care, Marital Quality, and Stress in Parents of Children with Autism Spectrum Disorders." *Journal of Autism and Developmental Disorders* 43 (2013) 2604–16.

Huyser-Honig, Joan. "All God's Children Have Gifts: Disability and Worship." Calvin Institute of Christian Worship. January 6, 2006. http://worship.calvin.edu/resources/resource-library/all-god-s-children-have-gifts-disability-and-worship.

Kinnaman, David. *You Lost Me: Why Young Christians Are Leaving Church . . . and Rethinking Faith*. Grand Rapids: Baker, 2011.

Myers, David G. *The American Paradox: Spiritual Hunger in an Age of Plenty*. New Haven: Yale University Press, 2000.

Sweet, Leonard, and Frank Viola. "A Magna Carta for Restoring the Supremacy of Jesus Christ: a.k.a. A Jesus Manifesto for the 21st Century Church." Beyond Evangelical (Viola's blog), June 22, 2009. http://frankviola.org/2009/06/22/a-jesus-manifesto-by-leonard-sweet-and-frank-viola.

Taylor, Humphrey, et al. "The ADA, 20 Years Later." Executive summary. July 2010. http://www.2010disabilitysurveys.org/pdfs/surveysummary.pdf.

14

An Epistemology of Empathy

Jeff Tacklind, DMin

> There is no understanding without standing under.
>
> —*Leonard Sweet*[1]

I DON'T KNOW HOW seriously you take the meaning of names, but mine, Jeff, means peacemaker. For the longest time, my parents feared that they had misnamed me. I guess this is because I tend to ask too many questions. Even as a child, I never bought simple answers. I pulled against common opinions. I still do.

But not simply for the sake of stirring the pot. Instead, I see danger in the absence of tension. The idea of compromise usually means that no one is getting his or her first choice. It is settling for less. And though there is some truth to this, the appetite for truth and meaning are never properly satiated with that type of meal. Simple answers are ultimately unsatisfying, like settling for tofu instead of steak.

C. S. Lewis describes convenient answers by saying, "If you look for truth, you may find comfort in the end; if you look for comfort you will not get either comfort or truth only—soft soap and wishful thinking to begin, and in the end, despair."[2]

---

1. Samson, *Justice in the Burbs*, 94.
2. Lewis, *Mere Christianity*, 32.

Certainly we know what he is talking about. But I'm not sure the opposite alternative is any better. Social media is saturated with so much shouting and pontificating. I often cannot get past the volume level. Everyone trying to sound so erudite makes my eyes glaze over. I'm looking for the "word fitly spoken"[3] as Proverbs speaks of, not the loudest opinion. Real truth doesn't just cut, it cuts to the heart.

Genuine Truth Seeking

There is a necessary amount of effort required to get at the truth. It is often messy and requires an awful lot of work. It requires an ear to hear not only the subtleties, but also the internal character that can withstand being opposed without becoming defensive. We are usually poor at both listening and being contradicted.

G. K. Chesterton wrote:

> What we suffer from to-day is humility in the wrong place. Modesty has moved from the organ of ambition. Modesty has settled upon the organ of conviction; where it was never meant to be. A man was meant to be doubtful about himself, but undoubting about the truth; this has been exactly reversed. Nowadays the part of a man that a man does assert is exactly the part he ought not to assert—himself. The part he doubts is exactly the part he ought not to doubt—the Divine Reason.[4]

Fundamentalism has complicated truth seeking. It has blurred, if not erased, the line between personal reason and Divine reason. It takes every personal belief and makes it "thus sayeth the Lord." This creates tension, but of the wrong sort. These truth statements often simply cover up the huge abyss of self-doubt that should be commonplace for any finite creature.

I've developed a litmus test to evaluate who are genuine truth seekers. I look for people that both sides of a debate are claiming as their own, the writers and thinkers that avoid simple categories and bring illumination to the deeper issues. I look for the ones that seek truth with openness and humility, the ones that are comfortable with paradox. I've found this characteristic in writers like C. S. Lewis and G. K. Chesterton. And I've found it in Len Sweet.

---

3. Prov 25:11 ESV.
4. Chesterton, *Orthodoxy*, 55.

The First Encounter of a Truth Seeker and Finding a Whole New Way

I remember when the emergent church movement was just beginning. At first, it was spoken of only in hushed, even embarrassed tones. A friend had given me a copy of a popular "emerging" book at the time. This controversial work opened up a floodgate of questions I had been painfully holding back for years. The author mentioned his appreciation for Len Sweet, who had introduced him to many of the concepts he was exploring. That caught my eye.

Later, I attended a church planting conference for a fairly large evangelical denomination. Part of the program involved cautioning attendees about postmodernity and the erosion of truth. One of the recommended resources was a book by Leonard Sweet entitled *SoulTsunami*. The speaker stated, "Here is a guy who understands the dangers as well as the opportunities, and where we can all go from here." While the early emergent church was being pigeonholed as something negative, Len was being heralded by the opposing side as part of the solution. This drew me in. I realized he had to be a truth seeker.

As I began to explore Len's writings, I was relieved to find none of the soft soap of empty compromise. Instead, I found modeled for me a different epistemology. (A different way of considering how we know things.) It was one that "combined furious opposites and kept them furious,"[5] in Chesterton's language. This was writing that embraced technology without idolizing it, that thought progressively without the need to dismiss all elements of conservatism, that cherished tradition without being stuck in old paradigms, and that was incredibly relevant without being self-congratulatory. It was deeply committed to the church and yet open to considering different forms and ways of being the church. It looked both forward and backward and somehow held on to both at the same time. When I later heard about the opportunity to study under Len, I jumped at it.

During my studies, I filled up page after page of useful tidbits and strategies from Len. But most of what I've gleaned from him has been watching his mind work. Often the best takeaways are the statements that filled in the gaps or transitions, the moments where he was thinking out loud, seeing him interact with questions and the complexities of where the church was going. Honestly, my favorite quotes of his aren't the ones that

---

5. Chesterton, *Orthodoxy*, 95.

show up in any of his books, but instead are those pearls of wisdom and perspective that seem to come from his peripheral vision. Those are the ones that you hurry to jot down, because if you don't, they're gone.

One of the required texts Len prescribes to all his cohorts is *Personal Knowledge* by Michael Polanyi. This book is much like a user guide for the discussions Len facilitates. Polanyi provides a model for how to speak of what you know, yet cannot quite put into words. He describes how to leave our familiar home in such a way that when you return, you discover new things about where you originally started. It is an epistemology of leaving and returning, a way of thinking for the discontent, for those who seek truth. It was like water to my thirsty soul.

Knowledge, to Polanyi, isn't simply about acquiring information, but discerning revelation. It is demonstrated most clearly in the moments of inspiration of the scientist and the artist. Knowledge and skills that we acquired over time necessarily fade into the background, allowing us to see past them.

True knowledge must draw us back, through reflection, to our original lens of seeing, allowing us to go deeper and beyond it. Truth and discovery require more than interpretation, it requires immersion. Like a pianist, who does not learn mere information, but is formed through the repetitiveness of her scales. She experiences the way forward, she receives it. She does not merely learn "about" it.

This immersion requires constant movement. Imagine the symbol of infinity, a sideways figure eight. As our thoughts and reflections move from opposite poles, like a skater on the ice, the process of action and reflection makes deeper and deeper grooves, creating a larger and larger soul.

Pastorally Seeking Truth in a Whole New Way

There are several elements to this that have proven invaluable to me as a pastor, and more importantly, as a person. The first is the affirmation of the value of good questions. Knowledge, in this view, is never a point of arrival, but has a sort of continual hopefulness that looks beyond how we currently understand. We are constantly looking for more, but not in a way that diminishes what we have. It is like the man in Mark who says, "I believe; help my unbelief!" (Mark 9:24 NIV). Moving knowledge out of the category of "possession" and embracing it as a "process" forces a healthy humility and necessary empathy. To truly discover, we must listen carefully to what we don't fully understand.

Questions that spark deep emotions are to be paid special attention to. If the truth is elegant, it is relevant to ask why. If our reaction to a new truth is defensiveness and creates personal insecurity, this should be viewed as invitation for deeper exploration. Len Sweet and Polanyi have helped me see the immense value of not merely what we believe, but how we have come to believe it. As Len puts it, "There is no understanding without standing under." We do not learn by simply acquiring facts. We learn through deep participation.

But truth seeking is not only a personal quest; it is also a communal endeavor. We learn truth like a language. Denominations are our Christian tribes and are vital to show us how we came to believe what we do today. Understanding our tribes also helps us to understand others. Once we identify our first language, we can begin to learn to speak and even become fluent in another's language and culture.

I remember Len telling me, "I make it a fundamental principle of true conversation that I have no right to argue with you until I can state the case you are making to your satisfaction."[6] This is placing understanding above opposition. This posture not only helps avoid misunderstanding, but it fosters deep empathy. Truth seeking always trumps simply being right.

True empathy forces us to look deeper at our own convictions and how and why we hold them. It exposes our own anxieties and requires us to look more closely at not just our justifications for our beliefs, but also the fears and doubts that lurk behind them. As we pay attention to these elements, we can let go of our need for absolute certainty and embrace a true, and yet rightly humbled, confidence.

Alasdair Macintyre refers to this search for understanding as learning a second first-language.[7] This allows church leaders to join with others in the larger church without limiting ourselves to our narrow, tribal battles. The outside world is justifiably wary of a faith where churches live in continual opposition to one another. When we oppose those of our own faith who happen to disagree with us on a specific matter we often become repugnant to those on the outside looking in. We are waiting to be asked by them for an answer for "the hope within us" when in fact, we are only adding more fuel to the fire of their suspicions and doubts.

---

6. Leonard Sweet, in discussion with the author.
7. See Macintyre, *Whose Justice?*

The way of learning through deep, reflective listening offers incredible value in dealing with the diversity within our own church bodies. Everyone naturally resonates with some aspects of the church while also not quite connecting with other parts of the ministry.

The plurality of the body of Christ requires a certain amount of courage. To begin with, one must first accept that their particular way of worshipping God as revealed in Jesus is not the only way. Many people trip over this. They naturally think in terms like "us and them, inside and outside." It is common to think of oneself as seeing rightly and that those who are different than us within the church, to varying degrees, see God wrongly.

Too much or too little expression during worship, too much or too little preaching, too much liturgy, too little emphasis on the Spirit, not enough care for the poor, etc. And so we start a new church, a new stream, one that is finally going to "get it right."

But what if we were able to learn to value, and even speak the language of the different streams of Christian faith? What if we saw our diversity as a strength? What if we learned to embrace an epistemology that placed love as the highest goal and sought to see not only the strengths of others, but our own weaknesses as opportunities to move further along in sincerely following Jesus?

The philosopher, Ludwig Wittgenstein famously wrote, "Whereof one cannot speak, thereof one must be silent."[8] But in a diverse community, we gain more than just different perspectives. We gain the ability to name those things we previously lacked the language for. Other tribes often have the language to name those things in our lives we couldn't quite see, let alone understand. But if we stay in communion with them, we can name them, and we can grow further into Christ-likeness.

A Church That Genuinely Seeks Truth

I pastor a church that has made this a significant part of our vision, to embrace a plurality of streams of Christian faith and strive to be a diverse and unified body of believers. To be quite frank, it has been messy. But it has also been life giving for everyone involved.

The messiness, in our context, emerges from our discomforts; when we're exposed to something new and different. Our discomfort can quickly become a nasty irritation. We get annoyed with the behavior of the person

---

8. Wittgenstein, *Tracatus Logico-Philosophicus*, 189.

sitting next to us. We grow irritated with the style of the speaker, or the specific content or (lack thereof) in the message. Without a greater vision of genuine truth seeking, some become cynical and decide to begin to look for a new church. Admittedly, this philosophy of ministry can be a risky model for church growth.

But I'm seeing the healthy effects of this plurality in my own little church and it is a joy to watch the fruit that is being grown. It is an experiment in Christian diversity. It is a true opportunity for spiritual growth by being exposed to the various ways that God moves in people's lives instead of simply reinforcing what someone already assumes that they understand fully. It cultivates a greater appetite for truth. The fruit that this kind of freedom brings has an intoxicating effect. It offers a grand and unexpected hope in the glorious future that God has for all of us.

But again, it is messy. Dispelling fear and anxiety always is, and those emotions can easily give way to anger and resentment. But an epistemology of empathy embraces this mess and calls us to look beyond it. It sets our minds on things above. It seeks revelation and discovery; it seeks the truth beyond the debates and discomforts and leads us to the higher values that unite us. It is the "most excellent way" (12:31) that Paul describes in 1 Corinthians. It values love above all things, as Paul eludes, love that is even greater than faith and hope.

I've found that this way of being the church is uncommon today, and yet, it is nothing new. It is simply being the body of Christ as Paul describes it. I believe this is what people are longing for the church to be, what the church was always meant to be. It is moving us forward and yet, ironically, it fully embraces what came long, long, before us.

This way of immersing ourselves in multiple streams of Christian faith and spirituality provides unending opportunities for growth in discipleship. But again, this kind of self-discovery isn't always immediately pleasurable. It exposes us and strips us of our natural defenses. But this is often what we truly need God to do for us. It pulls us away from the shadows into the light. We are unable to remain behind our protective arguments and self-justifications. We are forced to engage a God that is much bigger than our preferences by engaging His followers that are often very different from us.

This is what God has been doing within me. Revealing to me where I've become stuck and where parts of my soul have atrophied. This is growing me. I've become bolder about stepping into my insecurities and providing leadership by jumping in first. With every plunge, God keeps beckoning me to come further and further in. As I do, I experience greater and greater personal freedom. Freedom from my self, freedom from my comfort and security, Jesus inspired freedom that enlarges my heart so that I can better love him and better love others that he has always loved. Even those who are quite different from me.

My greatest joys are when I see people from different tribes coleading or serving together. When I see people moving into areas where they lack confidence, watching God come in and meet them in new ways. Usually God meets them through another church member, and often it is the last person they would expect it to be. That is part of the brilliance of the Holy Spirit.

In all of this, I observe so much healing. People that have open wounds from previous church experiences are finding care from modern day "good Samaritans." Their fearful assumptions are disarmed and they learn to embrace the value of the unfamiliar. As I look at the process of confrontation that is leading to reconciliation, I see a new sort of peacemaking taking place. It is the kind that doesn't settle, but presses forward to something bigger, something greater than anyone originally had in mind.

Astrophysicist Hugh Ross describes the difference between peacemaking and peacekeeping. He says,

> Peacekeepers ignore or isolate those with different models; or in a call for unity on the important matters, they attempt to suppress differences and controversies. Peacemakers, on the other hand, seek to bring resolution to competing models, to differences, and to controversies. The biblical testing method provides the body of Christ and the scientific community with the tools to resolve, rather than paste over or cover up, controversies, differences, and competing models of interpretation.[9]

I believe that this kind of peacemaking requires a touch of the divine. It is the peace Jesus describes in John 14:27 when he tells the disciples, "Peace I leave with you; my peace I give to you. Not as the world gives do I give to you. Let not your hearts be troubled, neither let them be afraid." And with this peace comes revelation. But not the simplistic revelation of something new. Instead, the revelation of what was once familiar deepening and providing new understanding.

Is this progressive? Maybe. But it feels to me more like a rediscovery. To be taken away from our comforts allows us to look back at the

---

9. Ross, "Interpreting Creation."

assumptions that had distorted our understanding. And not to simply jettison our previous understanding, but to grow it, to enlarge it. To allow it to become more God-like.

I remember a response Len had to someone calling him a visionary. He said, "If its true that I am a visionary, I hope I am merely pointing people back to the vision of Christ."[10] I think that is exactly right. This is the mark of a genuine truth seeker in the way of Jesus.

Bibliography

Chesterton, G. K. *Orthodoxy*. New York: Lane, 1908.
Lewis, C. S. *Mere Christianity*. New York: HarperOne, 2001.
Macintyre, Alasdair. *Whose Justice? Which Rationality?* Notre Dame: University of Notre Dame Press, 1989.
Polanyi, Michael. *Personal Knowledge: Towards a Post-Critical Philosophy*. Chicago: University of Chicago Press, 1974.
Ross, Hugh. "Interpreting Creation: Part 3, The Scientific Method." Reasons to Believe (website), May 2, 2011. http://www.reasons.org/articles/interpreting-creation-part-3-the-scientific-method.
Samson, Will, and Lisa Samson. *Justice in the Burbs: Being the Hands of Jesus Wherever You Live*. Grand Rapids: Baker, 2007.
Sweet, Leonard. *SoulTsunami: 10 Life Rings for You and Your Church*. Grand Rapids: Zondervan, 1999.
Wittgenstein, Ludwig. *Tracatus Logico-Philosophicus*. New York: Harcourt, Brace, 1922.

---

10. Leonard Sweet, in discussion with his students, May 2007.

www.ingramcontent.com/pod-product-compliance
Lightning Source LLC
Chambersburg PA
CBHW062041220426
43662CB00010B/1599